The Secrets of the Black Belt Mindset

Turning Simple Habits Into Extraordinary Success

Wil Dieck

TMT Publishing

Copyright © 2015 by Wil Dieck

All rights reserved. No part of this publication may be reproduced, distributed, or transmitted in any form or by any means, including photocopying, recording, or other electronic or mechanical methods, without the prior written permission of the publisher, except in the case of brief quotations embodied in critical reviews and certain other noncommercial uses permitted by copyright law.

ISBN 978-1-956169-08-9 (hard cover)

ISBN 978-0-9963072-0-8 (paperback)

ISBN 978-1-63315-576-3 (eBook)

A Sincere Request

Thank you for choosing to read my book!

I'm a proud independent author and publisher, so unfortunately, I don't have any big budget or promotional materials.

If you've enjoyed the book or think others would, please show your support by leaving a review on Amazon. Here's the link:

https://www.amazon.com/dp/B00S5AT2II

Your feedback is incredibly valuable in helping me improve my writing and letting others know your opinion.

Thanks again - your time and effort are much appreciated!

Wil Dieck

P.S. If you have questions please go to my website - https://mindfulmindhacking.com/

You can communicate with me directly from there.

Unlock Your Inner Potential with 10 Success Affirmations!

Congratulations on taking the first steps to success!

Take your success journey even further with our FREE report of 10 Powerful Affirmations for Success.

Just scan the QR code or follow the link to grab your own copy and find out how these affirmations can help propel you towards maximum success!

https://mindfulmindmasteryacademy.com/10-powerful-affirmations/

Contents

What is This Book About?	1
Introduction	4
1. The Battle of the Minds	11
2. We All Start at White Belt	38
3. Conquering Beliefs	59
4. Breaking Past the Fear Frame	88
5. Overcoming Inertia	111
6. Developing a Burning Desire	132
7. Self-Direction	146
8. The Indomitable Spirit	165
9. Transformation	188
10. The Real Secret	202
About the Author	204
Other Books by Wil Dieck	205
Endnotes	206

What is This Book About?

First, this book isn't about the superiority of any "style" of martial arts. This book is about shifting the way you think, using some of the same tools as those who, after years and sometimes decades of development, possess a Black Belt Mindset. Using these tools, you can learn to overcome challenges and take on new projects as easily as a Black Belt slices through a board.

Since I started training in Judo and Jujitsu nearly 50 years ago, I've watched and trained with some of the best martial artists in the world, most who have never starred in any martial arts movie or have been featured in any martial arts magazine. What I've found is that although all "styles" have their strengths and weaknesses, it's the skill and, even more, the spirit or mindset of the martial artist that makes one style "superior" over another.

After studying both the martial arts and human behavior for the last 4 decades, I've concluded that this mindset, let's call it the Black Belt Mindset, can be developed and utilized by anyone, whether or not they study the martial arts.

In this book, you'll discover:

- The importance of taking control of the training of your subconscious mind...

- How to create goals that will take you to where you want to go...

- Why your present beliefs are holding you back and how to create the beliefs that will empower you to achieve your goals...

- How fears keep you from going after your dreams and the steps you need to take to push aside those fears...

- What you need to do after you've destroyed your fears to take massive action...

- Why it's necessary to build a burning desire and how to create one that will drive you toward success....

- How to stay on the path you've started...

- How to stay motivated no matter the obstacles you face...

- How to continue to build and rejuvenate your Black Belt Mindset throughout your life....

This book incorporates what I've learned on the training floor, what I've picked up from other master instructors, what I've learned from thousands of books and recordings and attending hundreds of seminars and over 40 years of the systemic study of human psychology, the mind and human behavior into helping you develop the type of mindset that most people only dream of possessing, the Black Belt Mindset.

While this book won't turn you into a black belt, it will help you develop the strategies and instincts that a black belt would use to face an opponent on the training floor as well as overcome any other challenges in their lives.

Just as a small shift on a tiny rudder will completely change the destination of a large vessel, a small shift in your thinking can take you to a whole different place in your life.

This book should help you in those small shifts. That way you'll no longer be pulled wherever the currents of life take you. Instead, you will guide yourself to the destination of your choice, the places you actually want to go.

Now it's time to start your journey.

Wil Dieck

Introduction

It was late 1982. I was a Cho Dan Bo, the Korean term for Black Belt Candidate at Kwon's Karate in San Diego, CA. I was looking forward to testing for black belt as soon as the next testing date was set.

A moment before everything had been perfect. Now I lay on the ground holding my leg, cursing loudly. My knee hurt like hell and had ballooned to about three times its normal size.

The next day, I went to see the doctor. He sent me to see an orthopedic surgeon. After taking some x-rays of my left knee, Dr. Pollock, the orthopedic surgeon, told me the unwelcome news. I had torn the medial menisci. I needed surgery.

The good news was that Dr. Pollock was a pioneer of using arthroscopic surgery and had operated on some of the San Diego Chargers Football team with excellent results. He told me that within a few weeks after the surgery, I would be able to run and train in the martial arts again.

The bad news was that I didn't have any health insurance. I was working as a bench tech for an electronics company but had cut my hours down so that I could attend college and train more.

Since I had worked full time before, it was fairly easy for me to increase my hours so that I could get my health benefits back. The very next day, I talked to my supervisor and began working full time a week later.

Meanwhile, I had to limp around for nearly two months waiting for my health benefit to finally kick in. As soon as I was able, I went to see Dr. Pollock to schedule my surgery. He scheduled it for three weeks later.

I was excited. I would be able to work out again soon!

The day for my surgery came, and I reported to the hospital as instructed at 6 AM. I asked the woman at the front desk where I was supposed to go. She looked at a sheet of paper on her desk and told me, "You're not on today's schedule."

After asking the woman to check again, I figured that there had to have been some kind of mix-up, so I went home, waited for Dr. Pollock's office to open, and then called to see what was going on.

The doctor's office told me that there was a problem with my health insurance and that I should call my insurance company. Back then it was very easy to mix up the paperwork because it was, well, paperwork, not on a computer like today. So, I called my insurance company.

My insurance company told me that my insurance was fine and said that since my insurance was just reinstated, there might have been a delay in the hospital getting the right paperwork. Long and short, they told me to re-schedule my surgery.

I remember thinking that I should wait a few days to make sure that the insurance company had sent the correct paperwork to the hospital. I actually waited about three weeks until I called Dr. Pollock's office again.

When I finally called, his office told me that Dr. Pollock's schedule was extremely full, and he was going to take a four-week vacation and the earliest I could be scheduled was three months later. More than a little disappointed, but I once more set my second appointment for my knee surgery.

Three months later, I showed up again at 6 AM at the hospital. Again, I talked to the woman at the front desk and again she looked at a sheet of paper and told me, "You're not on today's schedule."

I couldn't believe it! I knew my insurance was in order. What could have happened?

Again, I called Dr. Pollock's office and again they told me that the hospital had told them that there was a problem with my insurance. Again, I called the insurance company and again they told me my plan definitely covered my surgery and to re-schedule my surgery.

Once more, I re-scheduled my surgery, this time for two months later.

Two months later, I showed up again at 6 AM at the hospital. Just like before, I talked to the woman at the front desk. I thought I was in the movie "Groundhog Day" as she looked at a sheet of paper and told me, "You're not on today's schedule."

This time I was really angry and asked the woman who in the hospital I could talk to at the hospital about this. She told me I needed to talk to the records office, but they wouldn't be open until 9 AM, so I went home.

But instead of going back to the hospital that day, I waited about a week and then finally went to the records department. I angrily told the woman behind the counter my issue. She went to the back to pull out my paperwork, looked at it and told me with a bit of a sneer, "The reason you're not getting your surgery is you're not covered."

Looking at her in disbelief, I told her that my insurance company had assured me several times that I was covered. She pointed down at her paperwork and with an even bigger sneer, told me, "That's not what it says here!"

Since I didn't have a cell phone (remember what it was like when there were no cell phones?) I asked, "Can I use your phone?"

She looked at me and with a very condescending tone told me, "No. That's against our policy."

I looked at her and angrily said, "I'll be back!"

I went home and again called my insurance company. This time I talked to the woman on the phone for nearly 45 minutes. Again, she assured me in no uncertain terms that I was covered and that I should go back to the hospital records room and find out what was going on.

Again, I went back to the hospital records room. This time another woman pulled out my paperwork and told me, "It says you're not covered here, but let me look at your insurance card."

I handed the woman my insurance card. About that time, the woman I had talked to before came in and started to say something to the woman who was helping me when the second woman exclaimed, "I see the problem. You have a new insurance number."

What had happened was that the number the hospital was using was the insurance number they had assigned me before. They assigned a new number after my injury, but since I had the same insurance company, Dr. Pollack's office thought that everything was the same as before. Only it wasn't.

A bad insurance number had delayed my surgery for nearly nine months!

This is a great example of what can happen when you put old, outdated information into a system. With the wrong information, a system can't work right, it becomes dysfunctional.

The system simply doesn't do what it was designed to do.

That's the same thing that happens when you allow old, outdated information to run your mind. It can't work right. At best, it functions at a level a long way below its capacity. At worst, it doesn't work at all.

When the hospital records room updated its information, it could do what it was supposed to do. With the new insurance number, I could get my surgery. Two months later I did and 18 days after that I was running again.

When you replace old, outdated thoughts and images in your mind, you can regain its functionality.

About the time I injured my knee, I was investigating hypnotherapy and Neuro Linguistic Programming as methods that could improve my personal and professional life. I must admit that at that time they were just some things I dabbled in.

Since then, I've earned my master's level belt in Tang Soo Do and Hapkido, and a couple of other Master's degrees in academia as well. I have been teaching martial arts professionally since the mid-1980's and am also a college professor teaching classes that pertain to psychology such as communications, group theory, social psychology, research methods and, of course, psychology.

I absolutely love to teach. That's why I started teaching martial arts.

When I started my martial arts school, I found that there were techniques from hypnotherapy and Neuro Linguistic Programming that could help my martial arts students develop more focus, more confidence, and greater self-esteem. These methods could actually act as a huge shortcut to help my students develop the kind of mindset a black belt develops over years of practice and training.

That's what you'll find in this book. Methods, called Black Belt Mind Secrets, that will help you take shortcuts on the path to developing what I call the Black Belt Mindset. These shortcuts will help you blast through barriers that are all in your mind on your road to more personal and professional success.

That's the reason I wrote this book, to help people just like you develop the Black Belt Mindset so that you can shift your thinking and live the long, healthy and abundant life of your dreams.

Now let's move on to the training floor.

Chapter One

The Battle of the Minds

"Do not dwell in the past, do not dream of the future, concentrate the mind on the present moment." - **Buddha**

Lee Jun Fan was born on November 27, 1940, in San Francisco, California. His family was from Hong Kong and they moved back there in 1941, just in time for the Japanese occupation that he and his family had to endure for the next four years.

Although as a child he had been a talented actor and dancer, when he became a teenager, Jun Fan got caught up in Hong Kong gangs. A chance meeting with a now famous Kung Fu instructor focused him on learning the martial arts. He became passionate about Kung Fu and learned all he could before he returned to the U.S. to live with relatives around Seattle, Washington in the late 1950s.

After finishing high school, Jun Fan became a philosophy major at the University of Washington. About that time, he started teaching Wing Chun and after getting married, he moved his family to Los Angeles to teach martial arts. He also moved to LA because he wanted to try his hand out at show business.

In 1966 he got his big break playing the character Kato in the TV series the Green Hornet. Just twenty-six episodes later, the series folded.

Not long after, Jun Fan severely injured his back. His injury kept him from training but gave him time to come up with an idea for a TV show about a Buddhist monk wandering the west that he presented to network executives. Jun Fan thought he would be the perfect choice as the lead character in the series but TV executives thought that an Asian actor wouldn't able to pull in the audience needed to attract advertisers so they gave the role to the white actor David Carradine who played a half Chinese Buddhist monk.

Jun Fan searched for other Hollywood roles but the only ones he could find were the stereotypical, menial roles that were given to Asians at that time, so he left Los Angeles and returned to Hong Kong in the summer of 1971. There he signed a two-film contract with a movie production company. In the latter part of that year, they released his first major motion picture, 'Fists of Fury'.

Of course, by now you've figured out that the name Lee Jun Fan, known by most people is Bruce Lee, one of the most influential martial artists and martial arts movies stars of all time.

What you probably didn't know were all the obstacles Bruce Lee had to overcome in order to reach his goals. All the things he had to do in order to become a 'star'.

How did Bruce Lee achieve all this in only 32 years of life?

I believe he did it using what I call the Black Belt Mindset.

Lee Jun Fan took charge of his behaviors by understanding what motivated him. This motivation gave him the mindset needed to drive him to take massive action, chasing his dream no matter what obstacles confronted him. It was his mindset that allowed him to attain his amazing success.

If you understand this mindset, you can too.

Human Behavior and Motivation

"Our subconscious minds have no sense of humor, play no jokes and cannot tell the difference between reality and an imagined thought or image. What we continually think about eventually will manifest in our lives." - **Robert Collier**

Daily behaviors, what you do on a regular daily basis, are what transform a martial arts student into a black belt. This book is about how you can take charge of your behaviors because your daily behaviors are what will make or break you.

It's also about how to turn on your motivation switch on at will and keep it turned on. That's because in order to do those daily behaviors, you need to know how to motivate yourself to take the action you need no matter how inconvenient or hard it seems at the time.

The first part of this journey is going to introduce you to the study of the mind and human behavior. We also call this psychology.

The Science of Psychology

Throughout history people have been examining human behavior, but as a science Psychology is a fairly new. The modern scientific study of the mind and behavior began in 1879 when Wilhelm Wundt[1] first opened his experimental laboratory of psychology at the University of Leipzig in Germany.

Since then, psychologists have come up with hundreds of theories about how the mind works and why humans behave the way they do. Each theory has its own unique ways of looking at personality and motivation.

These differences can be confusing. This can cause people to think of psychology more as a philosophy than a science. It's actually a combination of both.

While psychology has many ways of examining behavior, there is one idea that most fields of psychology agree on. This is that we all seem to have two minds, one that controls our surface behaviors and one that controls all our other behaviors, the behaviors underneath the surface. The surface mind is known as the conscious and the other mind is known to psychologists as the unconscious or subconscious. Another way to think about the unconscious or subconscious is other than conscious processes.

What is the Conscious Mind?

The conscious mind is the rational, logical part of the mind, the part of the mind we love to believe that is in control.

But the truth is that if your conscious mind was in control, you could alter any of your behaviors any time you want, changing your behaviors as easily and effortlessly as changing your clothes.

If this was the case, you could do and be anything you wanted, right?

But you know it's not that easy. In fact, you know it's hard to start good behaviors and stop bad ones. Behaviors can seem difficult, if not impossible, to change.

Why can't you just "will" yourself to change?

Changing behaviors consciously seems difficult because, as researchers have found in study after study, much of what you do is out of your conscious mind's control. Most of what happens in your mind results from your subconscious thoughts.

What Are Other Than Conscious Processes?

Other than conscious processes or the "subconscious" is the part of your mind that operates below your normal level of waking consciousness. It's the part of your mind that blinks your eyes, digests your food, causes your heart to beat and brings air into your lungs automatically.

It's also the part of your mind that controls nearly all of your behaviors.

Imagine your brain as an iceberg. Your conscious mind is like the part of the iceberg that you can see above the surface. This is only about 12 percent of your mind.

The bulk of the mind, the subconscious mind, is the other 88 percent and like the iceberg, it's below the surface. It's the part you can't see.

Your Automatic Operating System

Your subconscious mind works like the operating system of your computer, out of sight, in the background.

Here's a simple example:

If you're over 16, you have probably driven a car. If you have, think about the simple task of changing lanes. Right now, close your eyes and imagine you're in the left lane and you want to move to the right lane.

Actually grip an imaginary steering wheel and go through the motions of changing lanes right now.

Don't read on until you actually try this!

Now changing lanes is a fairly straightforward process, right?

If you're like most people, you probably held the steering wheel straight, then cranked the wheel slightly over to the right for a moment and followed by straightening it out again.

It's really easy, isn't it?

No, it's not! If you did what I described above, you, like almost everyone else in the driving universe, got it exactly wrong!

The motion of turning the wheel to the right for a tiny bit, then straightening it out again, would steer you from the left lane straight into a ditch!

Why did this happen? It's because you were thinking about changing lanes consciously.

The correct motion for changing lanes is turning your steering wheel slightly to the right, then back through the center, and finally turning the wheel an equal distance to the left side. After that, you straighten the wheel out again.

Check this out the next time you drive.

While you do this simple task every time you get into the car, if you are forced to access the process consciously, you drive into the ditch.

This is an example of how the operating system called your subconscious mind works. It does incredible tasks like changing lanes in your car, quickly and easily, in ways that you are not even consciously aware of!

A Huge Storehouse of Information

Your subconscious mind is a vast storehouse of information that contains all the sensory information you've ever experienced. Every sensation you've seen, heard, touched, smelled or tasted are all stored in your subconscious mind.

Any time your conscious mind needs to understand the outside world, it goes to its subconscious database to compare what you've experienced and learned in the past to what you are experiencing at that moment. This is how you can tell if you like a certain food, person, or activity. Your conscious mind asks the subconscious for data to compare with whatever sensory information it's receiving.

What's interesting is that your conscious mind isn't even aware of most of these processes. Instead of rationally examining the information you're receiving, it allows the subconscious mind to sort through all the data.

This means you are constantly making decisions and taking actions that affect every aspect of your life with no conscious thought at all.

An Automatic System that Handles Routine Tasks

The truth is, you don't have any idea about most of the activity that goes on in your mind. In fact, you really don't have any conscious awareness of the vast majority of your brain's ongoing, everyday activities. Not only are you not aware of them, most of the tasks your subconscious mind takes care of are things you don't want to interfere with.

For example, when you breathe, you don't consciously direct every muscle that expands or contracts in your chest and abdomen to pull in and push out the air.

You don't consciously tell your heart to beat or your blood vessels to expand or contract.

When you walk, you don't consciously tell your muscles to pick up each foot and then put it back down for every step. You just do it automatically, without thinking about it.

Your subconscious mind handles all of these tasks for you and, when you actually think about it, you want your subconscious mind to take care of all that stuff.

Why?

Because the conscious mind can only keep track of about seven to ten things at a time.

If you tried to keep track of all your bodily functions or if you had to think about how to walk or write your name, your thinking would completely overwhelm your conscious mind. Even if it could keep track of all those tasks, it wouldn't have any time to do anything else.

Instead of interacting with the world and enjoying the life you're living, your brain would use all its capacity to keep you alive. This would give you the same quality of life as an ameba!

Your Hidden Power

"People are anxious to improve their circumstances but unwilling to improve themselves, they therefore remain bound." - **James Allen**

Your subconscious mind automatically directs most of your actions and all of your habits and has incredible, immense power. In reality, it is the boss of you.

From riding a bike, to tying your shoes, to guiding your car home while listening to a baseball game on the radio, your subconscious mind takes care of all these things automatically. It makes your life a lot easier.

Your subconscious mind also has hidden power, power that many people don't realize exists and most people never try to understand, let alone harness. But the greatest inventors, athletes, entrepreneurs and leaders all understand and utilize the power of the subconscious mind. In fact, most of these high achievers use most, if not all, of the methods you'll find in this book to achieve their goals and dreams.

These high achievers understand, just as you soon will, that, just like steering your car, your other than conscious processes steer your life and your actions. These also control how you experience your life's events and, as a result, control your future.

Your Main Processing Center

Think of your subconscious mind as the primary control center of your whole body.

Your subconscious thoughts affect your whole-body mind system, both internally and externally. Even though some parts, like heartbeat and breathing, usually operate all by themselves, many people have learned to control even these.

This is especially common with martial arts practitioners, for example, as long ago as 1500 years ago; Tibetan monks would sit naked before an icy stream all night on the edge of a 12,000-foot mountain cliff.

After years of training, they examined these monks to see if they had learned their lessons properly. To check how well they'd learned their lessons, they continuously wrapped their bodies in sheets doused in ice water.

For the "normal" person, this deadly mix of freezing temperatures, relentless winds, and painful ice would mean hypothermia, frostbite, and almost certain death. Yet, because of the mental and physical training these monks had received, they were able to use the power of their subconscious to raise their core body temperature.

As a result, each survived with zero pain or illness.

All thanks to the power of their subconscious minds.

To this day, Monks go through this initiation ceremony with the same results. They have harnessed the power of their other than conscious processes, training their subconscious minds to create warmth in their bodies, despite the external environment.

Modern Day Uses of the Subconscious Mind

"Whatever we plant in our subconscious mind and nourish with repetition and emotion will one day become a reality." - **Earl Nightingale**

What you believe you can or cannot accomplish is also part of your subconscious thought process.

If you talk to nearly any Olympic or professional athlete, they will all tell you that they "practice" their sport in their minds. They tap into the subconscious because they understand that's where their "instinctual" or habitual moves come from. Using this mental practice, they program their subconscious minds for success.

The great news is you can use this same technique to improve any area of your life.

If you know how to operate this process and steer it to your command, the possibilities it can give you are endless. On the other hand, if you don't know how to operate this process it can sabotage you, hold you back and even sink your success.

Everything in your life - from the types and quantity of the food you eat, the level of income you earn, your habits, both good and bad, and even how you react to stressful situations are all controlled by your subconscious mind.

Your life and everything you accomplish or don't accomplish is a direct result of your subconscious thoughts and beliefs. Many experts argue that it is the most powerful force in your life.

Your Own GPS System

"It is psychological law that whatever we desire to accomplish we must impress upon the subjective or subconscious mind." - **Orison Swett Marden**

Your subconscious mind is like a GPS system, guiding you towards your desired destinations. Just like a GPS system needs an up-to-date map to provide accurate directions, your subconscious mind relies on current information.

If the map in your GPS is outdated, it can lead you down slow and inefficient paths or even the wrong destination altogether.

Similarly, if your subconscious mind is relying on outdated or inaccurate information, it can take you in directions you don't need or want to go.

To ensure your subconscious mind works properly, it needs to be programmed with the most updated routes that will lead you quickly to your desired destinations. Just like your car's GPS, your subconscious mind needs constant updating to guide you effectively.

So, you want to make sure to keep your mental map refreshed so you can stay on track and keep moving towards your goals.

Where Does This Programming Come from?

"We cannot always control our thoughts, but we can control our words, and repetition impresses the subconscious, and we are then master of the situation." - **Jane Fonda**

Experts tell us that everything you've ever seen or heard is sitting somewhere in your subconscious mind.

No matter how distant, these memories can affect your current thoughts, decisions, and actions.

Your existing perceptions have been forming your entire life, beginning when you were an infant. As you experience life your subconscious mind soaked in information like a sponge.

Your subconscious mind learned many things, like when you cried a magical creature that you later learned was your mother would come to feed you or change you or burp you. It also learned that when you smiled, people liked you, especially that magical creature.

As you grew older, it began making up rules about your life and the people and things around you. For example, if learning was important to your mother, there is a good chance she would give you a reward, such as saying "you're so smart" when you learned something new.

Using that feedback, you made up the rule that "learning is good".

On the other hand, if you tried to ask your dad a question you and he "punished" you with words like "can't you see I'm busy" when your dad was doing something like reading the paper, this feedback helped you make up the rule "talking to dad is bad".

While neither of these rules was absolute, your subconscious made a quick connection that you relied on to make future decisions about what action you would take.

When you were very young, your subconscious mind accepted everything and rejected nothing. That's because you didn't have any pre-existing beliefs to contradict what it perceived.

Your subconscious mind simply accepted that all the information you received during your early childhood was true.

By the way, this is why there are age recommendations on video games and movies because young kids can't tell the difference between them and reality (we adults can also have those problems, but that's a discussion for a later time).

The Problem with Your Early Programming

"You affect your subconscious mind by verbal repetition." - **W. Clement Stone**

Your early programming came with some real baggage. Every time someone called you stupid, worthless, slow, lazy, or worse, your subconscious mind just stored the information away for reference.

You, like so many of us, may have also received messages about your potential or limitations based on your physical abilities, skin color, gender, or economic status.

By the time you were 7 or 8 years old, your subconscious mind had been programmed with a great number of beliefs, false and true, based on all that input from people in your life, television shows and movies you watched, along with many other environmental influences.

How Does This 'Old' Programming Affect You Now?

"Only one thing registers on the subconscious mind: repetitive application - practice. What you practice is what you manifest." -
Fay Weldon

Your subconscious mind contains vast stores of information. These stores of information you've been acquiring your entire life and are much more than your conscious mind could ever handle.

You may think that as an adult you can simply forget or discard any hurtful or untrue messages you absorbed during your early life, but it's not quite that easy. The reason is one of the most fundamental ways you give your experience meaning is through your beliefs.

You've stored your beliefs in your subconscious mind. They act to reinforce your motivation to work hard and accomplish the goals you set for yourself. They can also act to sabotage you if it was trained to think you are unable to achieve your goals.

You store these beliefs deep in your subconscious and they affect how you habitually think. They also automatically block any attempt you make to change.

The only time you actually notice this negative subliminal programming is when it limits your progress in creating a balanced, successful, and productive life.

For example, someone who has been told they are "shy" may have a difficult time making a loud K'ihap or Kaai[2] in a martial arts class. Their programming has told them they just aren't supposed to yell loudly around other people. Their k'ihap is limited by a belief that may have been true and useful at one time but has nothing to do with the person they are now.

Their old programming is holding them back.

The same goes for sparring. New students often struggle with sparring because they consciously think about it. On the other hand, black belts tap into the incredible power of the subconscious mind.

Sparring and Your Nervous System

Over time, a martial arts student learns to free spar and have fun at it. But in the beginning, at least for most students, free sparring can be very difficult and even traumatic.

Sparring gives a martial artist student fighting experience without risking major injuries. It's controlled fighting. The idea behind sparring is to teach a student to" fight" in a safe environment. This lets the student improve their skills, and nobody gets hurt.

The student learns to respond to different techniques so that, if the occasion ever occurs where they need to defend themselves, they won't panic and will hopefully come out on top.

The problem is, if you don't have a lot of experience, sparring can seem like everyone is trying to kill you. This can cause a lot of anxiety.

Coding and Decoding

When you free spar, you take in a lot of raw data. Then you have to code the information you take in.

How experienced is this opponent? How tall are they? Are they quick? Do they seem to be very strong? Do they favor one side of their body or kick with a particular leg?

Beginners have little experience coding this type of information. That's why beginners hesitate and often have a lot of difficulty. There's too much raw data coming in for them to analyze, and they don't know what to do with the data.

Black belts can spar in a relaxed manner. Over time, they have analyzed enough raw data and learned from it so that they are sure of their abilities. They use the sensations sent through their nervous system to take in the raw data and translate into information they can use to enjoy the experience of sparring.

They don't panic because they have enough experience to know what to expect and how to respond.

That's part of the Black Belt Mindset. Training the mind to make sense of the information it receives in certain situations.

How Your Brain Makes Sense of Information

Your brain does the same thing with all the raw information you take in every day, moment by moment through your nervous system. We know this raw information as sensations or what you see, hear, touch, smell, and taste.

Your nervous system sends those sensations to your brain, which makes sense of it through a process called coding. Your brain then uses your experience and the experience you've learned from others to make sense of what's actually going on.

It does all of this in less than the blink of an eye.

So, like a black belt sparring, if your experience has provided you with good information, you'll be able to make good decisions about what to do with the information you're taking in.

But if your experience hasn't been totally accurate, you may end up making a poor decision.

If a black belt makes an inaccurate assessment of their opponent, they quickly recode the raw data they take in and shift their strategy. They quickly develop a new mental sparring strategy.

The same goes for you. If you have coded information you've received in the past incorrectly, you can use the techniques and processes you'll find in this book to quickly shift the way you think about it.

This will help you make better decisions. Better decisions mean living a better life.

How Your Brain Makes Sense of Information

Your brain does the same thing with all the raw information you take in every day, moment by moment through your nervous system. This raw information is known as sensations or what you see, hear, touch, smell and taste.

Your nervous system sends those sensations to your brain which makes sense of it through a process called coding. Your brain then uses your past experience and the experience you've learned from others to make sense of what's actually going on.

It does all of this in less than the blink of an eye.

So, like a black belt sparring, if your past experience has provided you with good information, you'll be able to make good decisions about what to do with the information you're taking in.

But if your past experience hasn't been totally accurate you may end up making a bad decision.

If a black belt makes an inaccurate assessment of their opponent, they quickly recode the raw data they take in and shift their strategy. They quickly develop a new mental sparring strategy.

The same goes for you. If you have coded information you've received in the past incorrectly you can use the techniques and processes, you'll find in this book to quickly shift the way you think about it.

This will help you make better decisions. Better decisions mean living a better life.

Mental Sparring Strategies

When sparring, a black belt uses their experience so they can form a mental strategy of how to engage their opponent.

If their opponent spars with her right foot forward, they'll have a mental map of how to deal with that. If their opponent moves in a line, moving forward and then retreating backward, they will have a mental map for that.

Since they have a lot of experience sparring, black belts will use their mental maps to quickly decide what kind of strategy to use on the opponent they're facing.

You also have mental maps you use in order to make sense of the world. The purpose of these maps is to help you quickly make sense of what's going on. This helps keep you safe.

Social Psychologists call these maps schemas.

Scripts and Schemas

A schema is a mental map or your knowledge about the environment and people around you and what your relationship is with them. A schema helps you make sense of the world quickly.

Schemas about things you do frequently are called scripts. An easy way to look at a script is an automatic set of behaviors used in a certain situation.

For example, you may have a schema called "driving to work in the morning". You get in your car and wait your turn to get on the freeway. Then you crawl along in the second line from the right because it's your "lucky line" that always gets you to work on time.

You patiently let people into your lane as they put on their turn signal while silently cursing the cars that dart in front of you without even letting you know they were going to move. As long as nothing really important happens you get to work without thinking about it at all.

You have scripts like this for lots of different things in your life, from how you get up in the morning, to how to order food at a Chinese restaurant, to how you deal with difficult people. These scripts help you take in information quickly so you can make decisions more easily.

Scripts make your life a lot simpler.

Heuristics and Shortcuts

Because your mind wants to keep you safe, it develops sets of what Social Psychologists representational heuristics. A representational heuristic answers the question, "What is this and how does it affect me?"

You use your experience to quickly categorize what's going on. For example, you see a person coming up the street. Without even thinking about it, you analyze if they're male or female, whether they're tall or short and if they are a different ethnicity than you.

You categorize all these things in the blink of an eye.

You use this information to categorize quickly, based on your experience and your environment, the approaching person to determine if they are a friend or a foe. This helps you decide whether to get ready to say "Hello" to an old acquaintance or to prepare yourself to fight or run away.

That's the purpose of a heuristic. Using millions of years of programming it helps to keep you safe. This way, you can hopefully pass on your genes to the next generation.

Another name for a heuristic is a shortcut. Something you do automatically when you are in a certain situation.

How do you create these shortcuts?

By programming and reprogramming your mind.

Your Programming

"If you accept a limiting belief, then it will become a truth for you."
- **Louise L. Hay**

Why do you have the shortcuts you have today? It's because of your programming.

Every day you encounter new experiences. As you encounter them you look to your stored database to make sense of them.

As a black belt spars, they look to their past sparring database to let them know what to expect. Their programming then guides their sparring strategy.

You do the same thing as you go through life. As you encounter a situation you evaluate it based on what you have experienced in the past. This helps you quickly make sense of it.

Just as the black belt uses their evaluations of their sparring partner to quickly set up a sparring strategy, your evaluations of your current situation will guide your actions.

How Your Subconscious Evaluates Your Current Situation

Let's say you run into a situation at work where your boss comes to you at 10 AM, hands you a huge file and then says to you, "I need this report by 12 noon tomorrow and I don't want any excuses," then walks away.

You look at the papers in your hand. Although you've done this report before, you know it usually takes a lot more than the 8 work hours you have.

You now have to evaluate the situation.

If you've been having problems with your boss, you might think about this situation as a threat.

If you know your boss has been under a lot of stress from home lately, you might think they have something going on that's causing them to act a little un-rationally.

If you know your boss has been under the gun from their boss, you might think that they are the one feeling threatened.

Whatever scenario you make up in your mind is how you are going to evaluate the situation.

Where to you get this information from? You get the information from experiences stored in the database of your subconscious mind.

What You Seek You Find

Now do you know for a fact that any of the scenarios you decided on are true?

Of course not! You'll actually make it up. You'll hallucinate the scenario you've chosen is true and whatever scenario you decide will justify your subsequent behaviors.

Let's say you have decided that your boss really doesn't like you. Instead of checking the facts, your subconscious mind (that clever detective) would immediately go hunting through your memories and find other examples of why this boss and other bosses haven't liked you.

Maybe you said something awkward in a meeting, or you didn't get a report in on time a year ago, or you caught your boss giving you a "funny" look. Whatever it is, your subconscious mind will look into your past to find the answers you are looking for.

It will help you conclude that you're somehow "unlucky with bosses" or "not able to fit in with the corporate culture" or whatever you decide.

But is this true?

I would say almost definitely not. You just made it all up in your mind. You hallucinated it. These hallucinations programmed your mind to find your faults and bring you failure.

But it doesn't have to be like this.

Just as the black belt learns from their successes and mistakes while sparring, you too can learn to make successful evaluations.

You don't have to let your subconscious mind limit you. You can re-program your mind for success.

Becoming a Black Belt Takes Work

No matter how many martial arts books you read and no matter how much great information they have, in order to become a black belt, you have to go to the training floor. You have to work out.

The same goes for reprogramming your subconscious mind, it's going to take work.

Training Your Mind to Have the Black Belt Mindset

In his book, "Zen and the Martial Arts" Joe Hymas described a time when someone asked Bruce Lee, "What would be your defense if you someone attacked you and you hurt or killed your attacker?"

After taking a moment to think, Bruce Lee reportedly answered, "It just happened."

In other words, he had done it without thinking, without conscious control. He had trained his subconscious mind to automatically respond to an attack and it "just happened". That response came from practicing his techniques repeatedly until they appeared automatically.

This is also the way to develop the Black Belt Mindset. You need to practice developing your responses in your conscious and subconscious mind. That way, you'll have positive, automatic responses that move you in the direction of your goals and dreams.

That's what the exercises in this book are for. The exercises in this book were designed to help you quickly develop the automatic responses needed to acquire the Black Belt Mindset.

Just as you have to practice kicks, punches, locks and throws repeatedly to develop the physical skills of a black belt, you'll have to practice the exercises in this book over and over again.

You need to do the work.

Chapter Two

We All Start at White Belt

The beginning is the most important part of the work. - **Plato**

Martial artists, no matter the style they study, start at white belt.

One of the favorite things I like to ask kids when they first begin training is, "What's the difference between a black belt like me and you?"

It's amazing the answers kids can come up with but the most common are things like "You're stronger, you can do better kicks, you know more stuff, you're taller, you're older," kids come up with a lot of ideas about what makes us different.

Then I'll tell them, "The only difference between me and you is a little practice."

Then I tell them, "The white belt signifies innocence, a new beginning for every martial arts student. A long time ago, you would only receive one belt that you would put on every time you came to class. Then over time your belt would become dirty and frayed from being drenched sweat and sometimes even sprinkled with a little blood."

Usually, I take a brief pause here while the kids look at each other with wide eyes, then I continue saying, "Your belt would become darker and darker until after many years of training your belt would become black. At that time, they would consider you a black belt."

I let that soak in for a few seconds and then I drop the bomb and say, "I was a white belt once."

At first the students might seem a little dumfounded, but after a few seconds you can almost see the light bulb going on over their heads.

My Beginning

It was 1966 when I first stepped onto a martial arts training floor. I was 13 years old.

The class was being held at Portola Junior High school where I went to school. A few days earlier, I had read an announcement that there was going to be a Judo class on two evenings during the week. That's all I needed to know. I went home and asked my parents if I could join.

Bruce Lee had just started playing Kato on the Television show, "The Green Hornet". My brother and I watched together, amazed by his abilities. After watching these shows, I knew I wanted to be just like the guy who could kick the light bulb out of a hanging light seven feet off the ground.

While Judo wasn't the same as Kung Fu, I knew it was a martial art. That's why I signed up to study with Sergeant Tanaka, a U.S. Army Ranger and why I attended his very first class.

Over the next couple of years, I took Judo classes with Sergeant Tanaka and loved every minute of it. It was an amazing introduction to martial arts. Unfortunately, Sergeant Tanaka transferred to another base a couple of years later. That was the end of my Judo experience.

Many years later, after graduating from high school and serving six years in the U.S. Navy, I found Master Young Hyuck Kwon, a six-degree master black belt instructor in Tang Soo Do and Hapkido. I began taking classes with him, again starting as a white belt.

These beginning classes, along with many others, changed my life.

When I first started practicing Judo, I wanted to learn the "secrets" of self-defense. You see, it was the 1960s in California. I was a skinny little red headed white kid going to a school that had a predominantly black population. While I got along with most of my peers, it was hard at times.

There was a lot of racial tension at my school, and being small, I got picked on a lot, not just by the black kids but by everyone. I figured that by knowing how to defend myself, I wouldn't get picked on as much. While those Judo classes didn't keep me from being picked on, they taught me how to think about myself differently and, as a result, I didn't get picked on as much.

Changing how I felt about myself was why I took up martial arts again all those years later.

Why People Take Martial Arts

While many people, like me, start practicing martial arts so they can defend themselves, there are several other reasons people begin to train in martial arts. These reasons all fit neatly into a psychological perspective known as humanism and Abraham Maslow's hierarchy of needs.

Abraham Maslow was a psychologist and one of the founders of humanistic psychology. Humanistic psychology began as a reaction to Psychoanalysis and Behaviorism, two schools of thought that dominated the study of human behavior in the 1950s which focused on a person's unconscious motivations.

Instead of focusing, as Freudian Psychoanalysis did, on how one's experiences or relationships with one's parents drives a person's unconscious motivations or, as Behaviorist did, believing that all behavior can be conditioned in the same manner that you would train a dog, humanism focuses on the inner good in a person. Humanism tells us that over time and with the right experiences, a person grows and develops through a process Maslow called "self-actualization".

Maslow felt that all people have needs that can be viewed as a pyramid. At the bottom of the pyramid are basic survival needs such as hunger, thirst and the maintenance of the body.

At the top of the pyramid are spiritual or self-actualized needs.

The three levels in the middle are the need for safety, the need to belong and be loved, and the need to learn to be competent, gain approval, and excel.

Nobody would take martial arts classes if their basic physiological needs were not being met. You can't work out if you don't have enough food or water or you don't have a place to sleep.

Everyone starts because a need in the middle, the need to feel safe, the need to belong or the need to feel competent, is not being fulfilled. On the other hand, black belts continue to train because they are striving to reach the top level. They want to become self-actualized, to obtain the Black Belt mindset.

Safety, Security and More

Like me, many people start taking martial arts classes to feel safe and secure. You get picked on as a kid or feel threatened as an adult and you decide to take martial arts classes so you can defend yourself. There's nothing wrong with that.

Some people take martial arts because a friend is in the class, and they're invited to come along. They take a few classes and enjoy the camaraderie and the attention they get from the instructors and their fellow students. This meets their need for belonging and to be loved. As a result, they stay.

Some people just want to have a better self-image. They want to improve their self-esteem. They do this by achieving belt levels and improving their physical skills. Becoming competent in one area of your life can, and usually does improve your overall self-image and martial arts training can help you with this as it has countless others.

No matter why you start, as a result, students begin to feel confident, to grow and, as Abraham Maslow would say, self-actualize.

If the student continues down this path eventually, they'll become black belts. There's no way they cannot. But what's interesting is most never do.

Why Most People Don't Become Black Belts

While thousands of people take martial arts, very few stick it out and reach the level of Black Belt. Out of a hundred students, maybe two or three will actually reach black belt.

Why?

While there are many excuses, most people stop practicing martial arts because they don't understand their why. As a result, they lose their motivation.

Those students that become black belts understand their why, what motivates them and, as a result, they continue to grow and develop.

Uncovering Your Why

"Values provide perspective in the best of times and the worst." - **Charles Garfield**

Before you go anywhere in life, you need to understand your motivation. You must figure out what counts.

What counts is your why for accomplishing what you've set out to do. It's your motivation for getting up out of bed every morning and doing what you need to do.

You are driven to do what you need to do by your values, the things that are most important to you.

What Are Values?

Think of values as your priorities. Values are what matter most to you. They are the things you care most about in your life. Your values guide you and help you prioritize the events and people in your life. This prioritization allows you to invest your time wisely.

What does investing your time wisely mean? It means getting a high, as businesspeople would say, ROI or return on investment. It means getting the absolute maximum out of your time investment as possible.

Although there is no guarantee, the average life span of a person living in the United States is 76 years.

That can seem like a long time until you do a little math. 76 years breaks down to 27,759 days. You have more or less 27,759 days to accomplish whatever it is you want to accomplish on what Earl Nightingale termed as our wonderful vacation on earth.

A Black Belt understands that once a day is spent, it is gone forever. They understand unless you decide on what you are going to do with the time you've been given that day, you are wasting it. They understand that once time is gone, it's gone forever. As a result, they consciously choose how and with whom they invest their time.

The Value of Time

Everyone understands that time is unlike any other resource. You can earn more money if you go broke. If your body isn't fit, you can improve your physical fitness. If you mess up a relationship, it is possible to repair it.

But no matter what you do, you'll never get the time in your life back.

Unlike those other resources, once a day is gone, it is gone forever. That's why defining your core values is so important, so at the end of your life you can look back and know the time you spent was actually an investment in the things and people you cherish the most.

Pain and Pleasure - The Reasons Behind How You Invest Your Time

Everyone invests their time in one thing or another for one of two reasons; to avoid pain or to gain pleasure. What's interesting is that the same input can mean different things for different people. It all depends on the feedback you receive.

Where do you receive this feedback? From your 5 senses, in NLP we call this your modalities.

What is NLP?

"NLP provides a systematic framework for directing our own brain. It teaches us how to direct not only our own states and behaviors, but also the states and behaviors of others. In short, it is the science of how to run your brain in an optimal way to produce the results you desire." - **Tony Robbins**

Like martial arts, I've been studying NLP for a long time.

I first became acquainted with Neuro Linguistic Programming or NLP in the early 1980s while studying psychology at the University of San Diego. The Nightingale Conant Corporation had just put out a set of cassette tapes that explained how NLP worked and how to use it to enhance your life. I invested in it.

I became even more involved in the practice of NLP after reading about its possibilities in one of Tony Robbins' books.

His research inspired me to search for even more information about NLP and ways it could be utilized.

NLP has helped me personally in many areas of my life. Using techniques from NLP, I learned I shifted the way I thought about what seemed to be enormous obstacles in my life and turned them into steppingstones toward success, some of which you'll read about later in this book.

As a martial arts instructor, I found NLP techniques especially useful to help students improve such things as focus, concentration, or confidence. When a student was struggling with a technique or with a lack of confidence, I would use a few of the NLP techniques you'll find in this book to help them shift how they were thinking about whatever was blocking them, allowing them to move successfully through the situation they faced.

Because of its effectiveness, I nearly thought of NLP as magic. Over years of study, I've found that NLP is merely a very efficient method for using psychology to maximize your results.

Origins of NLP

Although Tony Robbins is often associated with NLP, it actually originated in the early 1970s when two men, a mathematician named Richard Bandler and a linguist named John Grinder, began working together in Santa Cruz. Their goal was to uncover the reasons some people found success in an area of life while other people failed or just barely got by.

The result was a study of human behavior called NLP.

What Does NLP Stand For?

As you already have read, NLP stands for Neuro Linguistic Programming. Here's a way you can think about it:

"NEURO" has its origins in the word "neurology".

Information from the outside world comes to you from your senses. This information is sent through your nervous system as thought patterns.

How you experience the world results from your thought patterns or how you think about things. If you understand how you think about things, you can learn to how to control your thought patterns. By understanding how to control your thought patterns, you can change how you experience the world. This is an essential part of the Black Belt mindset.

The same goes for another person. If you understand their thought patterns; you can affect how they feel about you and your ideas. This is how a teacher becomes a brilliant teacher.

"LINGUISTIC" has its origins in the word "language".

Besides having thought patterns, you also have language patterns. When you take in information from your senses, your mind uses your patterns to translate those sensations into information you can use to define them or words.

You use those words to describe everything you see, hear, feel, taste, and smell.

That's why certain words resonate with you better than others.

The same goes for other people. They have certain words that resonate with them better than others. When you understand which types of words resonate with them, you can communicate with them easier and more effectively. The more effectively you can communicate with others, the more effective you are in all areas of your life, both personal and professional.

"PROGRAMMING" comes from the world of computers.

NLP assumes your mind is like an extraordinarily complex computer. Like a computer, your programming affects your results; good programming gives you good results and bad programming gives you bad results.

Using NLP, you can tap into your programming and use it to give you the results you desire. You can also use it to tap into another person's programming and actually align with it. When you are in alignment, also known as rapport, you can better understand the other person and they can better understand you, improving every relationship you have.

Modalities - How You Take in Information

Any time you use your senses to see, taste, touch, hear or smell something, you are taking in information from the outside world. Then, when you want to put meaning to those experiences, you "re-present" them internally, again using the meanings your senses have attached to those experiences.

The qualities you associate with the images, sounds and feelings you experience, the way you take in store that information and then code that information in your mind using your senses are known in NLP as your representational system. These are also known as your modalities.

While you use all of your senses to see, taste, touch, hear or smell, most of the time you can define them in one of three ways:

The first is the visual modality or thinking in pictures.

The second is the auditory modality or thinking in words.

The third and final way is the kinesthetic modality or thinking in feelings, tastes and smells.

While you represent your experiences using a combination of all the above modalities, the truth is you, like everyone else in the world, have a dominant modality. This modality is the primary way you process information.

Knowing how you primarily process information can help you determine the best way to shift your representations of the world and how you experience it. Since your choice of words describes your thoughts, your choice of words will also point toward which representation system or modality you primarily use. The same goes for everyone else in the world.

What Language Do You Speak?

Imagine three people, all who are going to see the same movie. They all watch the movie, and you interview each one and ask them about their experience.

The first person tells you about seeing the exciting scenes in the movie. They tell you about watching the actor's expressions and all about how the cinematography made the movie bright.

The second person tells you about how the actors' voices portrayed their feelings. They might tell you about how loud the movie's volume was or how the sound of a person whispering to the person beside them had distracted them.

The third person tells you about how the explosion shook the room. They tell you about how they felt when the heroine found out that her boyfriend had cheated on her. She might even tell you that the movie made her feel like the weight of the world fell on top of her.

Each of these people saw the same movie, but they described it differently.

One was thinking about their movie experience in pictures, one in sounds and the third in feelings.

The same goes for you. Although you use all three modalities, most likely you primarily use one of them to make sense of your world.

Understanding Modalities

In order for you to make quick and lasting shifts in your thinking, you need to understand how you primarily process information.

Use the following information to determine your primarily processing modality:

Visually

A person who mainly represents information visually primarily pictures or visualizes images in their mind. Visual people learn by watching.

When they recall data from their mind, they see it in pictures and use these pictures to process that data.

When a visual person speaks, they'll use words such as:

Look, picture, focus, seeing, visualize, reflect, I, focus, illustrate, see, show, vision, watch, reveal, hazy, shine.

A visual person will use phrases such as:

"I see which you mean."

"Show me what you mean."

"It appears to me."

"He has a blind spot."

"I'm looking closely at this idea."

If you primarily use words and phrases like this, then you're primarily visual.

Auditory

A person who mainly represents information auditorily primarily hears sounds and/or listens to an internal voice. Auditory people learn by hearing.

When they recall data from their mind, they might think about a time someone was talking to them, or the sound of their voice, or hearing a song. They might even hear themselves talking to themselves.

People who process information auditorily notice the distinct qualities of sounds, such as the volume or how loud it is, its tone, how soft or harsh it is, a location in relationship to you, and its speed, just to name a few.

When an auditory person speaks, they'll use words such as:

Say, listen, tell, ask, loud, clear, remark, vocal, discuss, deaf, accent, audible, clear, vocal, quiet.

An auditory person will use phrases like:

"Music to my ears."

"Rings a bell."

"Hold your tongue."

"Loud and clear."

"That's all Greek to me."

"On the same wavelength."

"In a manner of speaking."

"That's a lot of mumbo-jumbos."

If you primarily use words and phrases like this, then you're primarily an auditory person.

Kinesthetic

A person who mainly represents information kinesthetically represents information by touch, smell, or taste. These people experience the world primarily through feelings. Kinesthetic people learn by touching.

These people feel their experiences in a particular location in their body.

Kinesthetic people often talk about their feelings as being in certain parts of their body. For example, people who are experiencing fear will say things like "I have a stomachache and my head feels light".

When a kinesthetic person speaks, they'll use words such as:

Touch, cold, pressure, heavy, rough, warm, solid, pressure, push, gentle, hold, solid, concrete, smooth, or tackle.

A kinesthetic person will use phrases such as:

"Hold on a second."

"Control yourself."

"Going to pieces."

"A cool customer."

"Thick-skinned."

"I can't put my finger on it."

"Heated argument."

"They don't follow me."

"I just can't grasp that idea."

If you primarily use words and phrases like this, then you're primarily a kinesthetic person.

Back to Pain and Pleasure

Using your senses and language, you translate experiences in your life into either painful or pleasurable ones.

For example, some people associate exercise with pain because it can be painful, especially in the beginning. After exercising, muscles can get sore, joints can ache, and these can make your life miserable for a few days.

These people associate exercise with pain.

On the other hand, people who have pushed through the initial states of exercise might find exercise pleasurable from many points of view. Their body feels good, they feel good about what they see in the mirror and they enjoy the compliments of people telling them how healthy they look.

These people associate exercise with pleasure.

Another example is relationships. People who have had an unpleasant experience in relationships might associate relationships with pain. People who have pleasant experiences with relationships would associate relationships with pleasure.

Same activities, very different associations, that's because you always have the choice of what means pain and what means pleasure.

You Make the Choice

As a human being, you have the choice of what is pain and pleasure in your life. You make these relationships using your modalities to associate what you feel about something at a gut level. If the association is strong enough, it becomes anchored and will bring up powerful feelings every time you have the same experience.

This can actually be a good thing. For example, knowing that if you touch a hot stove, it burns will keep you from touching a hot stove over and over again.

But sometimes those associations are incorrect or false such as "since my last relationship was bad, all relationships must be bad". On a conscious level, you know all relationships aren't bad. You might have even had a good relationship or two in your past, you just can't get past the mixed meaning that you've associated in your subconscious with relationships.

When an association has a mixed meaning that can mean both pleasure and pain, it can distort your thinking. That's why it's important to understand both your modalities and your values.

The Black Belt Mindset associates values that move you in the direction of your goals and dreams with pleasure and values that don't move you in the direction of your values as painful.

It's that simple, well almost.

Back to Values

What kind of values are we discussing here?

The following is a short list of values that may be important to you. There are many others you can add.

This list will help you get a clearer vision of what's most important to you. This will help you prioritize your time so that you can invest it in activities and people who are aligned with who you are and where you want to go.

Black Belt Mind Secret # 1 – Choose Your Top Values

First, remember that this is not a complete list. It's only a guide. You can use it to understand your core values and link them to pleasure.

This list will give you a basic understanding of how to motivate yourself to do the work that needs to be done.

First, go through this list and choose up the top 10 values most important to you:

Now that you have chosen the 10 values that you feel are most valuable, put a ranking beside each one, from the one that is most important to the one that is the least important.

For example, if personal growth is on your list and is most important to you, put a number 1 beside it. If wealth is on your list but is ninth in importance, then put the number 9 beside it.

After you complete ranking your values, then write a brief paragraph that explains why (remember you're looking for your why) this value is important to you.

For example, in the case of wealth, why is wealth important to you? Is it so you can have lots of toys? Is it to give to those is need?

Remember; don't judge your answers as to what someone else would want. Write why this value is important to you.

Values List		
Personal Growth	Accomplishment	Challenge
Determination	Imagination	Persistence
Open-mindedness	Money	Prosperity
Wealth	Abundance	Fame
Relationship	Sexuality	Education
Excellence	Knowledge	Community
Play	Adventure	Discovery
Family	Dependability	Faith
Spirituality	Sacredness	Calmness
Gratitude	Religiousness	Mindfulness
Health	Fitness	Vitality
Work	Teamwork	Credibility
Professionalism	Discipline	Balance
Making a difference	Service	Financial Independence

Your Starting Point

"There are two mistakes one can make along the road to truth... not going all the way, and not starting." – **The Buddha**

Alright, you've already done a lot of good work, congratulations! But this is only the start. You have a few tools you can bring with you onto the training floor. Valuable tools you can use in your training plan and get you ready for training.

Let's move on...

Chapter Three

Conquering Beliefs

"Whatever the mind can conceive and believe, it can achieve." - **Napoleon Hill**

He was an excitable kid, and his parents wanted to help him control all of that energy. When he was 11, they signed him up for Karate classes. Two years later, he decided to take on weight training. By the time he was 18, he managed to win both a major bodybuilding and Karate event.

His success opened the door for a few modeling opportunities and product endorsements and this local fame began building his dream of being in the movies. It was then that he set his goal to become a martial arts movie action star.

The best place to break into martial arts movies in the late 1970s was China, so he moved to Hong Kong. He had little luck with the Chinese cinema, so he moved to where all dreams of stardom begin, Hollywood.

As many star-struck actors found, the movie business didn't welcome him with open arms. Since he wasn't from the U.S., he could only find work like driving a taxi, laying carpet, delivering pizza and the old Hollywood standby, waiting on tables.

Times were tough. Sometimes, he slept in his car, but after getting a few small background roles, he landed a co-lead as the Russian opponent of an American karate student in the 1986 Chuck Norris classic "No Retreat, No Surrender."

Still unknown and working as a nightclub bouncer, he bumped into Menahem Golan in front of a restaurant and performed his famous 360-degree kick within inches of his face. Impressed, the well-known Hollywood producer invited the young martial artist to a meeting with him to talk about a part in an upcoming movie the next day.

He arrived on schedule, but Golan let him cool his heels in the waiting room for six hours before inviting him into his office. After a brief conversation, he gave the young aspiring actor the script for the movie Bloodsport and the opportunity to play the lead role. Of course, Bloodsport became an enormous success.

By now you've probably figured out that we're talking about Jean-Claude Van Damme the darling of martial arts movies in the late 1980s and early 1990s. JCVD still has a following and has recently (as of the writing of this chapter) co-starred with many other older action heroes in "The Expendables II" directed and produced by Sylvester Stallone.

How could Jean-Claude Van Damme continue to go after his dream of becoming a movie star after encountering so many obstacles and rejections?

It's because he was certain of his ability to become a star. He believed he could.

Beliefs

Napoleon Hill published the self-help and inspirational classic "Think and Grow Rich" way back in 1937. I have read his book over a dozen times and have listened to a recording of it at least twice that. His famous quote "Whatever the mind can conceive and believe, it can achieve" is both good news and bad.

It's good news because your beliefs can take you wherever you want to go. It's bad news because your beliefs can hold you back from ever doing or even trying to do anything.

As Henry Ford so aptly put it, *"If you think you can do a thing or think you can't do a thing, you're right."*

Beliefs Change

Our beliefs as individuals and as a society can change as time passes. For example, on January 13, 1920, an editorial in the New York Times stated," A rocket will never be able to leave the Earth's atmosphere."

The New York Times stuck with this belief for nearly 50 years. Then, on July 17, 1969, the day after the launch of Apollo 11, the New York Times published the following correction, "Further investigation and experimentation have confirmed the findings of Isaac Newton in the 17th Century, and it is now definitely established that a rocket can function in a vacuum as well as an atmosphere. The Times regrets the error."

While some of your beliefs will send you into orbit, other beliefs can stop you from even reaching the launch pad. The great news is that, just like the New York Times, your beliefs can change. The better news is it doesn't take a rocket launch to change them.

What Are Beliefs?

Beliefs allow you to move through the world. They give you a sense of reference.

A belief is a shortcut to something you feel certain about. It is a generalization you make about what something means.

For example, when you go into the kitchen and turn the handle on your water faucet, you believe that unless something has happened to the water supply, you are certain that water will come out of that faucet.

Why?

Because your experience has caused you to create a generalization that says with certainty, "When I turn on the water faucet, I will get water."

Now what happens if you bring a person from a remote area that has never seen a water faucet into your kitchen and ask them to get you a glass of water?

If there is a window, they might look through it to see if there was a pond or lake outside that they could scoop some water from. They might even go outside and look for a source of water. One thing that is for certain is they will never look at the shiny metal tube in the middle of the kitchen as a source of water.

Why? Because their experience taught them to create a shortcut or generalization that says with certainty, "Water only comes from a spring or well or a pond."

Once they learn that water can come from the metal tube, their shortcut rapidly changes, and they can turn on the water faucet and get the water they need any time they want. They, like you, become certain that, unless there is a problem with the water supply, you will get water when you turn the handle of the water faucet.

Here's a question: was there always water available?

Yes, of course, water was always available.

Why didn't the person from the remote part of the world understand that?

Their beliefs about the sources of water controlled their search. In the same manner, just like the people from the remote village, your generalizations limit how you experience your world.

The Power of Beliefs

"For those who believe, no proof is necessary. For those who don't believe, no proof is possible." - **Stuart Chase**

By themselves, your beliefs are neither good nor bad. In fact, many of the shortcuts you've developed over your lifetime make your life easier and help to keep you safe. Beliefs only become a problem when they limit your ability to take action or have you taken inappropriate actions, actions that move you away from your goals and dreams.

Anthropologists have documented stories about how a witch doctor can "hex" someone and, as a result, the person who was hexed breaks out with a rash, becomes ill or even dies. Others have documented stories of sick people who spontaneously become well by a shaman's touch or a wise woman's special concoction.

In our society, there are reports of people who are spontaneously healed of cancer. When asked how they got better, they simply reply, "I got better because I believed I could."

Beliefs also affect martial arts students. For example, in martial arts schools throughout the United States, students test for belt advancement about every three to four months. In many systems, at higher levels, students who are testing are required to break boards.

Some students break the boards, and others don't.

Breaking a board is actually a simple thing to do. It's a matter of physics, hitting the board in the right place with the right amount of force.

But if it was actually that easy, every student would break every board every time. While sometimes is just a matter of a lack of focus, not hitting the board in the right place because of poor aim or concentration, many times there's a lot more to it than that.

More often than not, not being able to break the board has to do with a student's belief. If they believe they can break the board, they break it. If they don't believe they can break the board, they don't.

The same goes for you. Your personal beliefs define who you are and what you can accomplish.

They can help you by focusing your thoughts and energy on what you want and help you break through to achievement and success. Likewise, limiting beliefs can block you from achieving even the simplest goals.

Limiting Beliefs and the 'Four Minute Mile'

"Man is made by his belief. As he believes, so he is." - **Bhagavad Gita**

For many years, there was an overwhelming belief in long distance running circles that running a 'four-minute mile' was humanly impossible. Some doctors and scientists proclaimed that trying to run a mile in less than four minutes would harm a runner's internal organs and a runner attempting to run that fast could actually die trying.

Nearly every long-distance runner accepted this belief and, as a result, no runner could break the 'four-minute mile' barrier.

Fortunately, Roger Bannister didn't hold that same belief. Roger Bannister was a long-distance runner at Oxford University who began running at 17. In 1947, he was one of the few runners in the world who believed that they could break the 'four-minute mile' barrier.

For the next few years, these runners trained, and some came very close to breaking the 'four-minute mile' barrier. Then on May 6, 1954, Roger Bannister did it. He became the first human being to break the 'four-minute mile' barrier, running it in 3 minutes, 59.4 seconds.

What's interesting is that within six weeks the Australian runner John Lundy lowered the world's record by a full second. What is even more amazing is that since then, over a thousand people have run the mile in less than a minute, including high school runners, starting with Jim Ryun in 1964.

Although it is not an Olympic event, to this day, the mile remains the only non-metric race distance in which the International Association of Athletics Federations (IAAF) recognizes a world record. On July 7, 1999, Morocco's Hicham El Guerrouj lowered the world's record to 3 minutes, 43.13 seconds, nearly 16 seconds faster than Roger Bannister's 1953 pace.

Sports Illustrated honored Roger Bannister as "Sportsman of the Year". Later he was knighted by the Queen. But his greatest contribution was showing us that once you take control of your beliefs, you can accomplish anything.

How Can Beliefs Affect You?

"It's not the events of our lives that shape us, but our beliefs as to what those events mean." - **Tony Robbins**

Psychologists love to study identical twins. Since identical twins have identical genes, psychologists believe that only environmental differences can account for differences in their behavior, so they look at identical twins to identify how the environment affects behavior.

Some of these studies involve identical twins who grew up with an alcoholic father. These studies start when the twins are kids and then follow them into adulthood.

What they found was fascinating. Often, one twin would become an alcoholic while the other would completely abstain from drinking any alcoholic beverages at all.

When asked about why they ended up the way they did, both gave the identical answer, "With the way my father was, how could I have done anything differently?"

Even with the same environment and identical genetic make-up, the twins ended up with completely different lives. So, it wasn't the environment, and it wasn't their genetics, it was their belief about drinking alcohol that affected their behavior.

One twin believed that because of their father, they couldn't escape becoming an alcoholic. The others believed that there was no way they would ever let alcohol control them.

They were both right.

What you believe directs your life. Like identical twins, your beliefs can send you down a non-constructive path or send you on the path to your dreams.

What Are Your Beliefs?

Many years ago, when I was first awarded my black belt, I doubted my skill level. Although I felt my skills were adequate enough to be a black belt, I didn't feel that my skill level compared with many other black belts I trained with.

One day, a friend I trained with brought over a videotape (yes it was a long time ago) of a recording he had made of some martial arts classes we had worked out in together. As I watched the video, the skill level of one of the black belts in the background amazed me. I tried to make out who he was, but he was too far in the back to recognize.

As I thought to myself, "Who could that stranger be?", the camera zoomed in on their face and, to my amazement, that black belt was me! I was that extremely skilled black belt in the background!

I watched that video a few more times, paying close attention to my block's punches and kicks. As I did my forms in the video, I watched. I saw I was sparring brilliantly.

From that day on, I was a changed man. That video had changed my beliefs and had shifted the way I viewed myself. I realized I had the skills to become an outstanding martial artist. When I look back, I believe it was right after viewing that video that I decided I could become a martial arts teacher. I decided I could because I was no longer held back by my limiting beliefs.

Examples of Beliefs

"Stop thinking trouble if you want to attract its opposite; stop thinking poverty if you wish to attract plenty. Refuse to have anything to do with the things you fear, the things you do not want." - **Orison Swett Marden**

Your beliefs are nothing more than a bunch of memories you've stored over the years. Some beliefs empower you, and some, like my belief of my martial arts abilities, disempower you.

For example, one student watches a black belt perform a flying kick, jumping over 5 students to break a board held tightly by two students and thinks to themselves, "I can't wait until I can do that!" The student sitting right next to them is thinking, "I'll never be able to do that."

Another example is when a student goes to break a board for the first time. As they watch the students before them, one student thinks, "Hey, that other student broke their board. I know I'll be able to break mine." The next student thinks, "I don't know how they can break that board so easily. I'll never be able to do that. I'm probably going to fail my test today."

Same events, but they had dynamically opposite beliefs and, as a result, experienced completely different results.

People who struggle with breaking boards, learning math, meeting new people struggle because of the beliefs they have about themselves. Often that belief is similar to the belief I had about my abilities as a black belt, the belief that "I'm not as good as other people, they are all better than me."

If it wasn't for that video shifting how I saw myself, I may have stopped training and never would have become a teacher. You can also change images in your mind to change your beliefs and you don't even need a video.

You can shift your beliefs using your representational systems.

Representational Systems

Your senses take in information from the outside world through your nervous system. Your brain translates the information into things you see, hear, or feel. It attaches meaning to those inputs and helps you make sense of the world.

While everyone uses all three representational systems, you probably, like most other people, use one system more than the others. The system you use most often is known as your dominant system.

Here's an example. Close your eyes and think about a sunrise. How do you represent that image?

Do you see the sun coming up in the sky in the east, chasing away the darkness and replacing it with its golden rays? If this is how you primarily represent a sunrise, your dominant representational system is your sight. You are primarily a visual person.

Did you hear the sounds of the birds chirping, people moving around and other early morning sounds? If this is how you primarily represent a sunrise, your dominant representational system is your hearing. You are primarily an auditory person.

Did you feel the warmth of the rays of the sun on your face, feel the early morning breeze, or smell a fresh cup of coffee? If this is how you primarily represent a sunrise, your dominant representational system is how you feel things in your body. For our purposes, this can include what you smell or taste. You are primarily a kinesthetic person.

While each of these ways of representing the world is different, none is superior. The reason it's important to understand how you primarily process information is because by understanding how you process information; you can shift how it appears to you.

By shifting its appearance, you can change what the information means to you. This is how you manage your beliefs.

Certainty and Uncertainty

If you believe that something is possible, you are certain about it. This is called certainty in NLP.

If you don't believe or have doubts that something is possible, you are uncertain about it. This is called uncertainty in NLP.

If you are certain, you can do something, you will work on it until it's done. If you doubt you can do something, you'll either give up at the first sight of obstacles or you won't even attempt it.

Although you don't have to be 100 percent certain that you can accomplish everything you attempt, if you are more certain than uncertain, you will at least try something. As you begin to succeed, your certainty makes it much more likely you won't quit.

When you are certain, you see, hear, and feel a certain way about the thing you are certain about. You understand certainty through your representational systems.

For example, let's say I ask you, "Is the sun going to come up tomorrow?"

Your mind may represent that certainty either by saying "yes" either silently or out loud. You may nod your head in agreement or feel a certain way in your stomach. You may immediately see an image of a sunrise.

Somehow, your representational systems let you know you are certain that the sun will rise tomorrow. Understanding how you know you are certain is important because once you know how you represent certainty, you can use those representations to help you through the difficulties you'll encounter when trying something new.

What Do Submodalities Have to Do with Certainty?

When you answer the question, "Is the sun going to come up tomorrow?" Your mind might see the answer as a picture of a sunrise. If you do see the sunrise as a picture, is it a big picture or a small one? Is it in color or is it black and white? Do you see it right in front of you or is it to the left or right? Is it a still photo or a movie?

If your mind represents the answer as a voice that says "yes" is the voice high or low pitched? Is it in front of you or to the left or right, or even behind you? Is it your voice or someone else's voice, such as a friend's or your parent's? Does the voice have a specific tone? Is the sound near or far away?

If your mind represents the sunrise as a feeling, is the feeling heavy or light? Is it a sharp feeling or a dull one? Where in your body is that feeling? Is there a temperature associated with that feeling?

In NLP, we call these distinctions submodalities. Submodalities are the composition of how your mind represents the input of sights, sounds and feelings your senses give you.

How to Understand How Your Submodalities Represent Certainty

Understanding your submodalities isn't that hard, but it will take a little work.

Ask yourself the question, "Is the sun going to come up tomorrow?" then invest as long as you need to go through this list of submodalities, using the descriptions on the right to figure out how your mind represents certainty to you (Leave uncertainty alone, you'll be working on it next):

Let's start with Visual:

Visual	Certainty	Uncertainty
Color or Black & White		
Size		
Close or Far Away		
Blurred or focused		
Bright or Dim		
Depth (Flat or 3D)		
Associated or disassociated*		
Framed or Borderless		
Movement (Still frame or Movie)		
Speed of Movement**		
Number of Images (Spit Screen. Etc.)		

*Associated means you are seeing the scene through your own eyes, as if in the image. Disassociated means you are looking at yourself, watching as if in a movie.

**Speed meaning is it at normal speed, faster than normal or slower than normal.

Next, let's look at auditory.

THE SECRETS OF THE BLACK BELT MINDSET

Auditory	Certainty	Uncertainty
Volume 1 = low 10 = high		
Stereo or mono		
Do you hear words or sounds?		
Pitch		
Speed of sound*		
Tonality (soft or harsh)		
Location ins space (front, back, etc.)		
Rhythm		
Duration		
Timbre (fulness of sound)		
Continuous or discontinuous		

*Speed of wound meaning is it at normal speed, faster than normal or slower than normal.

Finally, kinesthetic.

Kinesthetic	Certainty	Uncertainty
Location in your body		
Intensity (1 – 10)		
Pressure (hard or soft)		
Temperature (hot, cold, etc.)		
Texture (Smooth or rough)		
Pulse rate		
Breathing rate		
Duration (how long does it last)		
Shape		
Moving or in one place		

Now that you know how your mind represents certainty, think about something you are uncertain about.

For example, if you answer the question "What am I going to do after work (or school) today?" your answer may be, "I'm not sure. I might go by the store to pick up some groceries, I might go by the gas station to buy some gas or I might just go straight home."

The answer to this question is uncertain. In other words, the answer is "maybe I'll do this or maybe I'll do that." Whatever your answer is, it is bound to be measurably less certain than your answer to "Will the sun come up tomorrow?"

To understand your differences, you're going to go back and compare how your mind uses your representational systems to present the answer to you.

Think about the image your mind represents to you when you answer the question, "What am I going to do after work (or school) today?" Now go through each of the submodalities above just as you did for certainty and note your answers next to each one.

Now don't just read this section and go on. If you want to develop the mindset of a black belt, you need to finish this exercise before going on.

Shifting Your Beliefs

Remember what happened to the student who didn't believe they could break the board? They didn't break the board. Their belief told them it wasn't possible.

Would that same student believe that the sun would come up tomorrow? Unless some type of psychological disorder affected them, they would be certain, beyond a shadow of a doubt, that the sun would rise in the morning, just as it has since the beginning of time.

What if they could take that same certainty and apply it to breaking the board? Would they break it? Of course, they would, and they would break it easily!

You can do the same thing. Using the knowledge of what makes you see, hear or feel certainty about something, you can shift your beliefs and break through the barriers that, in the past, held you back.

Conquering Your Beliefs

Black belts have no doubt they can break boards. Years of training allow them to use their submodalities to quickly snap into certainty and easily break the boards.

Unconsciously, they use these same submodalities to access certainty when faced with challenges in other areas of their lives. This ability to snap into certainty is why black belts will attempt and seemingly easily accomplish things that intimidate others. Using their submodalities, they have built a direct path to that part of their brain that holds their sense of certainty, allowing them to quickly access it to take on any challenge they face.

You are using this same path to certainty right now. Only you use it to access certainty that your problem is going to be with you today, tomorrow and in the foreseeable future. You are using your submodalities to be certain that your problem is permanent and you are powerless to change it.

Focus on What You Want

In order to get rid of what you don't want, you have to focus on what you do want. This is the only way you're going to change, by getting fed up with what you whatever it is you want to be rid of, whatever is holding you back and then replacing it with what you actually want.

Since your present belief is that this is going to remain a problem in your life, perhaps forever, you continue to focus on your problem. That's why it's still here.

Your belief about that problem is represented similarly to your belief about the sun coming up tomorrow. You are certain it exists. That's why it looms so large in your reality.

The way to make it have less power over you is by using your submodalities to represent it the same way you think about something you are unsure of. This way when you ask, "Is this a real problem?" your mind will think, "Maybe yes, maybe no."

Black Belt Mind Secret #2 – Shrinking Your Doubts

Black Belt Mind Secret #2, the rapid belief exchange or "WHOOSH" technique, uses your submodalities to shift how you represent a limiting belief in your mind. This changes your problem from a belief of "that's an enormous problem I'll never be rid of" to "that's no big deal".

You do this simply by exchanging your limiting belief for a more empowering one.

The great thing is you won't need years of training to master your submodalities; you can use the following steps to snap into certainty any time you wish:

Rapid Belief Exchange (The WHOOSH Technique)

1. Think about a limiting belief that looms large in your mind, something you believe will be with you for a long time, or perhaps forever. This might be "With my background I'll never be able to get a job that pays what I want to make" or "With my looks I'll never be able to attract someone into my life" or "I don't think I could ever become a black belt."

2. Use your imagination and create an image of yourself with your present belief.

Imagine how you look. See yourself with this belief. Are your shoulders hunched? Is your chin down? Are your eyes focused on the ground? Go through all the visual submodalities you worked on in the previous exercises to create a picture of you in this state.

Imagine what you feel. Does your stomach feel "funny"? Does your neck and back hurt? Do your legs feel weak? Go through all the kinesthetic submodalities you worked on in the previous exercises to find out what you feel like in this state.

Imagine what you hear. Who is telling you that you can't succeed? Is it you or someone else? What does that sound like? Are there loud sounds that keep you from hearing how you can succeed? Go through all the auditory submodalities you worked on in the previous exercises and hear the sounds that are calling to you into this state.

3. Use your imagination and create an image of yourself with the empowering belief you would prefer.

Imagine how you look. See yourself with this belief. How do you hold your shoulders now?

Is your chin up?

Is your back straight?

Is your gaze straight ahead?

Go through all the visual submodalities you worked on in the previous exercises and create a picture of you in this empowered state.

Imagine what you feel like.

Are you feeling "strong"?

Are your shoulders relaxed?

Do feel "centered"?

Go through all the kinesthetic submodalities you worked on in the previous exercises and feel what it's like in this empowered state.

Imagine what you hear.

Who is telling you that you can succeed?

Is it you or someone else?

What does that sound like?

Where is it coming from?

Do you hear inspiring music?

Go through all the auditory submodalities we discussed above and hear all the sounds that are calling you to be in this state.

4. Now imagine that you're seeing this image on a huge IMAX 3D movie screen that is in the center of your imagination. You're experiencing this movie with all your senses because they have added a fourth dimension to this theater, the dimension of feeling. You can actually touch, smell, taste and see and hear everything in this movie.

Let this entire image, with all its submodalities, take up the whole of your consciousness. Allow yourself to bathe in these images, taking in every detail, hearing the wonderful voices and sounds, enjoying the feelings, the smells, the tastes.

Now shrink this image down to the size of a small black box. Use your imagination to pull it down to the lower left corner of the screen. As you pull it into the corner, shrink it until it's a small black dot. Now let that small black dot rest on the bottom left corner of the screen.

5. Now close your eyes and allow the image of you not believing in yourself and all those submodalities to appear on that huge IMAX 4D movie screen located right in the center of your imagination. Involve all your senses. Let it momentarily become your reality.

6. As you say the word "WHOOSH" as loudly as possible, use your imagination to expand that small black dot in the left corner of your movie screen, quickly and rapidly. That 4D image of you is growing and expanding until it takes over your

entire consciousness. Your consciousness is now filled with this new 4D image of you.

Allow yourself to see, hear, feel, taste, and smell everything that is around you.

Take everything in.

Enjoy it!

Revel in it!

Bask in this new glorious image of you!

7. Shrink the image of the new you down again. Turn it back into that small black dot on the bottom of the screen. As the new image shrinks, let the old image of you not believing in yourself fill up the screen.

8. As you see, hear, feel, taste and smell everything around you in the old image of you not believing in yourself, adjust your submodalities to make the images less intense until they barely affect you at all.

If the picture is bright, make it dull.

If it's in color, make it black and white.

If the sound is loud, turn down the volume.

If it's your mother's voice, turn it into a cartoon character's voice.

If you feel pressure on your neck or back, relax your neck or back.

If your stomach feels "funny" get it to feel "normal'.

8. Again, as you say the word "WHOOSH", use your imagination and allow that small black dot in the left corner of your movie screen to grow, quickly, rapidly. That 4D image of you

has grown and expanded until, taking over your entire consciousness. Let your consciousness fill again with this fabulous new 4D image of you.

9. Turn up your submodalities to make the image brighter, the sounds crisper, louder, the voice more pleasing. Feel those feelings of the new you, the tastes, the smells are now so pleasing.

Let this image take over all your senses and as you experience this say out loud, "Yes!" Pump your hands and arms into the air above you and repeat "Yes" again loudly four or five more times, each time pumping your hands and arms into the air.

10. Repeat this process as many times as you need until you can overcome uncertainty, knowing you can achieve what you want instantaneously.

Maintaining Your New Belief

Some people struggle to maintain their new belief. Instead of being steady, their new belief behaves like a cork in the water, floating in and out between certainty and uncertainty, depending on the type of input you're getting at the moment.

In order to steady your new belief, you can use a technique known as anchoring. Anchoring is used to solidify or anchor your new beliefs and behaviors.

Anchors are nothing new; in fact, you are being affected by some sort of anchor every day.

They are simply learned or conditioned responses to a certain stimulus. You can create an anchor in the same manner you create any conditioned response, by associating a neutral stimulus to an unconditioned response leading to a conditioned response.

Let's review how to instill a conditioned response.

You order a pizza. You receive the pizza in a pizza box (the neutral stimulus).

You open the box, smell the pizza, and salivate (drool). That's your body's unconditioned response to pizza. Nobody had to teach you to salivate at the sight of pizza. You did it automatically.

Let's say you're a big pizza lover and you order pizza every day for a month. By the second week or so, you'll begin to salivate as soon as you see the pizza box.

In fact, you might even start to salivate as soon as you hear the pizza delivery guy's car pull up, but for this illustration, let's assume you live where you can't hear the car pull up. The door opens and as soon as you see the pizza box, you begin to salivate.

This is known as a conditioned response.

In NLP terms, the pizza box has become an anchor that elicits the conditioned response to salivate. This leads to Black Belt Mind Secret #3.

Black Belt Mind Secret #3 - Anchoring Your New Belief

As you already know, besides the three basic submodalities of sight, hearing and feeling, there are two additional submodalities: smell (olfactory) and taste (gustatory).

Smell and taste are powerful. They are so powerful they can instantly bring back memories.

For example, the smell of chocolate chip cookies can bring you back instantly to the kitchen where your mom or grandmother used to bake them. So can the smell of baking bread. That's why real estate agents sometimes bake cookies or bread in the kitchen at an open house. They know it will trigger that conditioned response of thinking about home (smart huh?).

When used with your other submodalities, these two submodalities can help you anchor certainty into place, allowing you to access certainty instantly.

Here's how you can anchor certainty (or anything else):

1. Let's say you want to be certain that you can break the boards at your upcoming belt test.

Create that image of your belief that you can break the board onto your huge IMAX 4D movie screen. Create certainty around the belief that you can break those boards.

2. Now you're going to associate a neutral stimulus with your belief. To do this, you're going to think of a smell (or taste). For example, think of the smell of orange blossoms (to help you with this exercise smell an orange as you do this).

As you bring that image of your belief that you can break those boards into your consciousness, imagine the smell of orange blossoms (take a whiff of the orange). As you smell it, imagine how your nostrils are being affected by the sweet orange scent in the air.

Maybe you can imagine tasting the sweet orange nectar as it slips over your tongue and tickles your throat.

You might even see the word "orange blossoms" printed in big bold letters floating across a movie screen in your imagination.

3. Now that you've conditioned your response, check how it works. Think of your new belief and then imagine the smell of orange blossoms.

4. Rapidly repeat this process six or seven times.

5. Now think of your new belief and the smell of orange blossoms. What you'll find is, just as you started salivating at the sight of the pizza box, you'll have anchored that image of certainty along with your new belief.

Just don't make pizza your anchor.

Using Rapid Belief Exchange Technique in Everyday Life

Now that you've gone through the rapid belief exchange technique, you can now put yourself in your desired state simply by closing your eyes and imagining the taste or smell of orange blossoms or whatever smell or taste you've decided.

This quickly shifts the way you experience your belief. By shifting the way you experience your beliefs, you shift your thoughts about how true and permanent those limiting beliefs actually are.

You can use this same process to shift the level of your belief in anything. You can boost your beliefs as well as diminish them.

With practice, you'll be able to shift how you represent any of your limiting beliefs. It's this shift that will help you break through your limiting beliefs and strengthen the Black Belt Mindset.

Just like the runners before Roger Bannister found out, a belief doesn't have to be real to block your achievements. A "mere belief" can keep you from accomplishing your goals and dreams.

What's important to remember is you are in control of your beliefs. You are in control of your thinking.

When you take charge of your thinking, exchanging beliefs that hold you back for ones that empower you, you quickly begin to shift your life's direction.

This shift allows you to find gaps in those old barriers. You might even find that those old barriers didn't even really exist.

It's these shifts in your thinking that allow you to create a new, more empowering reality, one that will rocket you in the direction of your goals and dreams.

Chapter Four

Breaking Past the Fear Frame

Kids picked on Carlos a lot because he was shy, wimpy, and a scholastically mediocre student. He wasn't much of an athlete and since his family moved around constantly, it made him a target for the school bullies.

After graduating from high school, he joined the Air Force and in 1958, he went through and graduated from Air Policeman training. After graduation, they stationed him at Osan Air Base in South Korea.

In Osan he began training in Tang Soo Do (Korean Karate) with Jae Chul Chin[3]. When Carlos' enlistment ended, he moved back to Southern California, where he opened his first martial arts school.

In Korea, Carlos enjoyed competing against other martial artists. When he returned to the U.S., he hoped to prove his skills against American competitors. In 1964, he suffered a sound defeat by Joe Lewis (twice voted the greatest fighter in karate history) in his first U.S. karate tournament. He returned the next year only to be defeated again, this time by Allen Steen, who also defeated Joe Lewis that year.

Not one to give up easily, Carlos continued to hone his fighting skills and in 1967 he came back to win the tournament, beating Joe Lewis, Skipper Mullins, Arnold Urquidez, Victor Moore, Ron Marchini, and Steve Sanders.

Early the next year Carlos was beaten by Luis Delgado, but he went back and worked on developing his skills. By year's end he had avenged his defeat by beating Delgado, winning the Professional Middleweight Karate champion title which he held on to for the next six years.

After winning the 1969 Triple Crown, Black Belt Magazine awarded him Fighter of the Year. During his stellar fighting career, he won at least 30 major tournaments until finally retiring from competition in 1974.

Carlos, also known as Chuck (a name he picked in the Air Force) has also been a martial arts movie and TV star, and yes, his last name has always been Norris. He is a martial arts legend.

How did Chuck Norris go from being picked on as a kid to a karate champion? It was simple; he learned to face his fears. He understood that facing his fears was the only way he could learn to overcome and move through them.

"Always do what you are afraid to do." - **Ralph Waldo Emerson**

In most martial arts systems, students learn to spar (to fight in a safe, controlled environment) within the first few months of their martial arts training. While most students will tell you they look forward to sparring, in reality, most are at least slightly afraid. While their mouths say that they are not afraid, you can see this fear in their body's reaction to the situation. You can actually see their acute stress response (stress is your body's natural reaction to something you are afraid of) being activated.

What's the acute stress response?

You've probably heard of the acute stress response by its more common name, the fight-or-flight response. The fight-or-flight response is simply what gets your body ready to fight or run away in a situation your brain believes to be dangerous.

Your Body's Response to Fear

There are actually three responses to fear, to fight, to flee or to freeze. Besides fighting or fleeing, your mind can tell your body to freeze, to hold its position so the predator that is stalking you can't see you. This is because most predators' eyes are designed to notice movement. When you freeze predators have a hard time finding you with their eyes.

Your body goes into one of these three responses because your mind slips automatically into a pattern that's thousands of generations old. It acts this way every time your mind believes you are in danger. It does this to keep your gene pool safe.

It doesn't matter which of these three physical responses you choose, fight, flight or flee, what happens inside of your brain is exactly the same. When you first note the threat, your hypothalamus (a pea sized portion of your brain located at the top of your brain stem) instantly activates two systems, the sympathetic nervous system and the adrenal-cortical system.

Your sympathetic nervous system activates the adrenal medulla (the inner part of the adrenal gland) which activates your adrenal glands, triangular shaped glands that are on top of both of your kidneys. Your adrenal glands then release epinephrine and norepinephrine, two highly potent hormones, into your bloodstream.

While your sympathetic nervous system kicks into high gear, your hypothalamus also releases corticotropin-releasing factor (CRF) into your pituitary gland (a small gland attached to the bottom of your hypothalamus by a slender stalk called the infundibulum). This activates your adrenal-cortical system, which releases another thirty or so hormones into your bloodstream.

This witch's brew of highly concentrated hormones is like red bull on steroids (no pun intended). They cause your heartbeat and respiration to speed up, your blood pressure to skyrocket, and your muscles to become tense and ready for action. Your sympathetic nervous system does all this to get your body physically ready for the threat.

But there is a problem. The problem is that even though these drugs (hormones are drugs made naturally by your body) have done all the right things to get you ready to fight, flee or freeze, if your mind isn't able to handle the threat your body will fly into overload.

How Fear Affects Sparring

If you watch martial arts students that are new to free sparring, you can see how fear affects them. You can actually see their respiration increase.

Some begin breathing so rapidly and shallowly that they become lightheaded. As a result, these students need to sit down.

Fear also increases the sparring student's heart rate.

While your heart needs to beat faster to get your body ready for a threat, too high a heart rate actually does just the opposite. In his book, "On Killing," former army Lt. Colonel Dave Grossman says that you are operating optimally when your heart rate is between 115 and 145 beats per minute. Grossman goes on to say, "After 145 bad things begin to happen. Complex motor skills begin to break down... At 175, we begin to see an absolute breakdown of cognitive processing... the forebrain shuts down and mid brain–the part of your brain that is the same as a dog's (all mammals have that part of the brain)–reaches up and hijacks the forebrain.[4]"

Your forebrain is the part of your brain that takes in information from your physical senses and then tries to make sense of it. Your forebrain is also responsible for controlling your body's motor functions. These processes become impaired when your heart rate is too accelerated.

Above 175 beats per minute, your body hardens its outer shell. While this makes it harder for sharp weapons to penetrate your skin (it also reduces the bleeding that would occur from any cuts or gashes), it also makes it your muscles rigid. Rigid muscles respond in a slow, clumsy manner. This hinders your ability to throw effective kicks or punches.

This natural fear response is why beginners don't do well at sparring. In order to spar effectively, you have to learn how to control your automatic response to fear. Black belts have learned how not only to control this fear response but to actually harness it, so it benefits their sparring.

Aren't We Born With these Fears?

Any child psychologist will tell you that children are born with two basic fears: the fear of falling and the fear of loud noises. You learned your other fears. All fears you have besides those two basic fears you picked up along your path of life.

When I tell this to a group of people someone will inevitably ask during the presentation or come up to me afterwards and ask, "What about the fear of snakes?" or "What about fear of the dark?" or whatever fear they have.

My answer is always the same. You learned that fear.

How do I know?

It's because there are people who have never had any fear of snakes, spiders, the dark or even giant rabbits or dwarfs. If a group of people do not have that fear, that implies that the fear of whatever "it" is you are afraid of is a learned fear.

Studies About Fear

There have been many studies done about fear in primates. Studies have found that monkeys that are born in the wild are afraid of snakes. This seems to make sense since poisonous (and some non-poisonous) snakes will bite and then eat monkeys for dinner.

When scientists raised a monkey in a laboratory, the monkey didn't react negatively when it saw a snake, poisonous or not. They are not innately afraid of snakes. This leads researchers to conclude that they learn this fear from the monkeys in their troop[5].

Monkeys in the wild learn to fear snakes just like you learn nearly all your fears, from cues you get from others close to you. These fears are not part of your genetic makeup.

Studies About Fear

Fears result from your leaned responses to people and events in your life.

For example, as a child, you may have been afraid of the dark. From a psychological point of view, the fear of the dark makes little sense. As an embryo, you lived in the dark for nine months. If you turn off the lights in a room, babies do not seem to mind the dark. In fact, turning off the lights is one way to help a baby relax and go to sleep.

So where did the fear of the dark come from?

The fear of the dark starts in the pre-school years, at around 2 or 3 years old. It's a product of a child's imagination. This is an age when the child is old enough to imagine, but not wise enough to distinguish fantasy from reality. It's the fear of the bogyman, witches, goblins or whatever else the child imagines it might be.

Television shows, movies and books teach you that "bad things" live in the dark. In fact, there are many stories that may have been written to motivate the children to go to bed using darkness as the motivator.

Since you are being told, repeatedly by many different sources, that bad things happen in the dark, you begin to believe it. You are afraid of the dark because it's 'natural 'to be afraid of something you 'should be' scared of.

You learn that the dark holds things you can't see, things out there you don't know about. Now you believe that the dark holds evil things that are there to harm you. You've learned to fear the dark.

You may even hold on to this fear of the dark into adulthood, refusing to go into a dark room or walk around the neighborhood at night, even if you live in a crime free neighborhood! It has conditioned you to fear the dark.

Conditioned Fears

Your other fears are also conditioned. For example, if you fear speaking in front of groups, it's because you have been conditioned to fear speaking in front of groups.

It could be that somewhere in your past you received feedback that made you believe you were 'shy'. Maybe someone introduced you to a new adult, and you didn't know what to say. To cover up for your social faux pas, your parents might have said, "Oh she's just shy".

This happens a few more times and then every time you meet a new adult person, you grab your parents' leg and hide behind it. You are now officially afraid of meeting strangers.

Maybe when you were in first grade, you raised your hand and gave the wrong answer. The result was a lot of snickering and finger pointing from your classmates. Because you were adventurous, this may have occurred several times until you finally linked talking in class to being laughed at and humiliated.

Now, when asked to speak in front of a group, you start to sweat, your hands shake, and you stutter incoherently. Just more proof that you are afraid to speak in front of groups.

You weren't born with these fears. It's just like how the monkey learned its fear of snakes. You learned your fears, and that's good news! Since you learned a fear, you can unlearn or replace it with a more empowering mindset, the same way a black belt does.

Black Belt Sparring

When a black belt spars, their acute stress response stays in check. While the same hormones will flow throughout their body, increasing heart rate and respiration along with everything else it's supposed to do, it keeps them all operating in the optimal range that Dave Grossman talks about in his book.

How is it that the black belt can control their acute stress response?

They keep their fears in check the same way they learned them, through conditioning.

A Bit About Breathing.

When a martial arts student begins to spar (or do just about anything else) we constantly remind them to breathe. Successful martial arts instructors don't just remind students to breathe, they show them how to breathe. To optimize their oxygen supply, they bring their breath deep into their lungs using what's known as diaphragmatic breathing.

Before we go on, let's discuss the two basic types of breathing: diaphragmatic and costal.

Diaphragmatic breathing works in the abdominal area. This is the type of breathing we find in babies and is the type of breathing people naturally experience when they are sleeping or deeply relaxed.

Diaphragmatic breathing uses your diaphragm to bring air into your lungs. Your diaphragm is a dome-shaped sheet of muscle that goes all the way around the bottom of your rib cage, separating your chest from your abdomen.

When your diaphragm contracts, it descends. This makes room for your lungs to expand and air to fill them. You know you are breathing with your diaphragm when your stomach rises and falls with your breaths.

Costal breathing works by opening and closing of your rib area. Using this type of breathing, you are only breathing into the upper part of your lungs. This leaves over fifty percent of your lungs uninflated and without air.

If you use this type of breathing exclusively in a highly stressful event, such as sparring, your lungs will rapidly run out of air. This will rob your body of the fuel it needs to continue to operate, oxygen.

This can cause you to hyperventilate or pass out.

This is why many beginning martial arts students quickly run out of energy. They don't have enough energy to burn. Their breathing doesn't bring enough oxygen into their bloodstream.

Black Belt Mind Secret #4 - Belly Breathing

Black belts have learned how to control the physiological aspect of their acute stress through the use of diaphragmatic or belly breathing. Through practice, black belts have formed the habit of allowing their diaphragm to bring them the oxygen and energy they need when sparring. This helps to prevent their body from taking over their mind.

Here's how you can make belly breathing a habit:

1. Put one hand lightly on your stomach and your other hand lightly on your chest.

2. Take a gentle breath in through your nose, drawing the air deeply into your lower lungs.

3. Without trying, let your belly expand. Don't put any effort into its expansion. Just let your lungs fill with air.

The air will also fill the upper portion of your lungs. Only the hand on your belly should move, not the hand on your chest.

4. Exhale slowly through your nose. Feel your stomach contract as you breathe out. Make sure you push all the air out of your lungs. You should take slightly longer to exhale than to inhale.

5. Continue to take in and let out your breaths slowly, paying attention to the expansion and contraction of your belly. At minimum, take five to seven breaths.

6. Practice, practice, practice! Practice belly breathing at home, at work, when you go shopping, everywhere you go. In a short while, you'll begin using diaphragmatic breathing automatically.

The wonderful thing about this technique is you can quickly learn how to calm your body and mind anytime and anywhere.

It's More Than Breathing – It's Your Frame

While it would be nice and simple if all you have to do is control your physiology (breathing pattern) to control your fears, there's a lot more to it than that. In order to have instant control over your fears, you need to control your frame.

What Are Frames?

"Whether you think you can or think you can't - you are right."
- Henry Ford

A frame has been described as "a general focus or direction that provides an overall guidance for thoughts and actions during an interaction." In psychology," frame" refers to how we look at the world as in the frame of reference.

An easy way to think of the word frame is how the world appears to you.

For example, let's say you are looking at photos taken at a picnic. When you look at the photos, the first thing you'll search for is you.

Why?

Your image gives you a frame of reference about the photo. For example, where it was taken, who else was at the picnic, what time of the year and day it was taken, etc. Your frame of reference helps you put the photo into perspective.

More than just information about who, what and where, your frame also lets you know how you felt about the picnic and the other people there and why you felt that way. Your frame helps you make sense of a situation.

Your frame also directs what you pay attention to, what you focus on. This is why your frame is so important for controlling fears. It directs your focus.

Race Car Driver Focus

Danica Patrick was the first female NASCAR driver to win a NASCAR Sprint Cup Series pole ever. The internet company, Go Daddy, sponsored her because she was an amazing race car driver.

At the Indy 500, the average speed is between 218 and 225 miles per hour. To put that in perspective, a jetliner only goes about 155 miles per hour at takeoff. With wings, those cars could actually fly!

During a race like the Indy 500, you'll see cars often pass in the area between the wall and another car. Race car drivers call this the gap.

If you were to put a camera inside Danica Patrick's helmet you would see that as she's passing her eyes only focusing on one thing, on the gap between the other car and the wall.

If you were to take a racing course, you would learn that the reason Danica's eyes stay focused on the gap is because she knows her car will go in the direction of her eyes. She would run into the wall if her eyes focused on the wall. She would slam into the other car if she focused on the other car.

That's why she focuses on the gap. That's where she wants to go. She knows the only way she can pass a car safely while close to the wall is to focus on where she wants to go.

We can say the same for you. Your focus pulls you in its direction. If you focus on your fears, it will pull you in their direction.

Just as racing car drivers learn to focus on the gap, to where they want to go, you need to learn how to focus your thoughts on what you want instead of on what you fear.

The Power of Questions

Your mind is always looking for answers. It wants to know why things are the way they are. So, it makes up questions about the world and everything in it. It's a questioning machine.

For example, if you are looking for your keys, you might ask, "Where did I put my keys?"

This question will guide your focus to where you left your keys. If you don't see them where you think you last put them, you'll go looking for them at all the usual places you might drop them.

If you still don't find them, what will you do? You'll ask yourself, "Okay, what did I do when I got home?"

You'll come up with "I picked up the mail. I went to the bedroom and hung my jacket up in the closet. Oh yeah, my keys are in my jacket pocket!"

Your questions guided your focus to where you left your keys. They helped you come up with the answer you needed to find them.

Simply put, your questions guide your focus. Your focus frames your answers.

Why Beginning Sparring Students Don't Spar So Well

Beginning students don't spar well. You might think, "Well, that's obvious. They don't have enough experience to spar well," and you'd be right.

Since they don't have a lot of experience, they haven't learned to breathe very well. We've already gone over that.

Another thing they don't do well is control their focus. They don't ask themselves the right questions.

Typical types of questions a beginner might ask themselves are, "What happens if I get hurt?" or "What if I fail to do well and look really stupid?"

These questions presuppose that their sparring experience is going to be a negative one. That's why they don't do well; they have already decided that they won't.

Your Presuppositions Influence Your Outcomes

If a race car driver would have a presupposition that they were going to drive at 215 mph into the wall, how long would they be a race car driver? How about if they presupposed they would hit the other car?

I hallucinate to say that no person would remain a race car driver with these types of presuppositions. That's because it would always focus them on the bad things that could happen, the things they don't want.

Just like the race car driver who focuses on the wall or on the car they are passing, the beginner's questions focus their mind on things they don't want. Since the beginner is focused on "not looking stupid" or "Not getting hurt" they react defensively to the other student's techniques.

As a result, they feel stiff and uncomfortable. Their mind tightens their body and they never get into the flow of the match.

Some students get so uncomfortable that they quit. Their focus has taken them to a place where they never see themselves as successful at sparring and, as a result, not having fun and no one is going to continue training in the martial arts unless they feel they are having at least a little fun.

What Happens When a Student Gets Some Experience?

If a student wants to improve their sparring, they have to improve their focus. How do you do this?

By asking better questions!

Better questions empower you. They allow you to pattern your thoughts in a manner that gives you a better outcome.

Instead of asking disempowering questions, a more experienced student might ask themselves, "Is this person right-handed or left-handed?" Another basic question they might ask could be, "Okay, when I sparred this person the last time, what was their most used technique?" or "Does this person rely on speed or are they more of a power sparer?"

If they feel themselves tensing up, they might ask, "Am I breathing correctly?" or "Do I need to slow down my breathing?"

By asking better questions, you come up with better answers. These answers frame your thinking about the situation as "under control". This allows you to relax so you can respond smoothly to your opponent's attacks.

Black Belt Mind Secret #5 – Controlling Your Frame

Your pattern of thinking, your frame, controls your focus. With the right frame, you have more control over your outcome. Use these steps to practice controlling your frame:

1) Control Your Physiology

For your sparring, or anything else to improve, the first thing you need to do is take control of your physiology. If your heat beat rises above its optimum level, it will hijack your thinking, causing your mind to race out of control. This is why you practice deep breathing.

You can use this type of breathing in any situation where you find your respiration and heart rate rising, such as in a meeting at work or during an exam at school. No matter what you are doing, belly breathing can help to bring your physiology back under control. Only after your physiology is under control, can you take charge of your focus.

2) Ask Better Questions

Now that you have taken back control of your physiology, ask yourself questions that empower you, questions that frame your situation in a useful manner.

At the beginning of a sparring match you might ask, "What new techniques have I learned recently that can I try out today?" or "What one technique would I like to improve today?"

Asking these types of questions focuses your thoughts on learning and improving rather than on what could go wrong. Your questions pattern your thinking and help control your frame.

Again, you can do this in a meeting at work or while taking an exam. If a meeting becomes a little heated, you can ask, "What do we all want to achieve at this meeting?" or "What could get us all focused on our desired result?"

This focuses your mind on your desired outcome. We know this as an outcome frame. We'll talk more about this a little later.

3) Shift Your Thinking Pattern

Asking better questions shifts your thinking pattern. When you shift your thinking pattern, you change your frame.

The Frame You Can Use to Break Past Fear

Now that you know Black Belt Mind Secret # 5, how to control your frame, which frame should you choose to break past your fears? While there are countless frames, there is one frame that can help you move past fear quickly and easily.

We know this frame as the "outcome" frame. What makes it so powerful is it directs your focus to take you in the direction you want to go.

Outcome vs. Problem

"Live out of your imagination, not your history." - Stephen Covey

You're going to run into issues in your life. When these issues come up, there are always two frames you can choose from, the problem frame or the outcome frame.

A problem frame focuses on the past, what went wrong, or who or what is wrong. Another way to describe the problem frame would be to call it the blame frame. Who or what is to blame for this issue?

There are many common questions that are problem focused. For example, when you run into difficulties, you might ask, "Why can't I do this?"

If you examine the question, you'll notice that it presupposes that you cannot do whatever "it" is.

Another problem focused question when you run into difficulties would be "Why are obstacles always getting in the way?" The presupposition here is that obstacles will always appear.

The problem frame focuses on things outside of you, such as "What caused me to mess up?" or, "Who can I blame?" Focusing on the external will always thwart your efforts because you have given control to something outside of you. Problem frame questions focus on why you can't achieve your goals.

The opposite of the problem or blame frame is the outcome frame. Like the race car driver that focuses on the gap, the outcome frame focuses your imagination on the desired result, what you want.

An outcome frame allows you to see the possibilities life brings you. It helps you frame those possibilities in a way that brings you the energy and resources you need to accomplish your goals.

Just as poor questions focus you on the problem, the right questions can help you focus on what you want, your outcome. Instead of asking "Why can't I do this?" you can ask "How can I get what I want?"

As the Bible says, "What you seek, you will find." Just as the race car driver uses her focus to guide her car into the gap, outcome-based questions guide your mind to search for what you want.

Other examples of outcome-based questions are "What do I want?" or "What do I have that can help me succeed?" If you are struggling for answers, you can ask, "Who can I ask for help?"

These questions focus you on accomplishing your goal by developing a solution. They focused your attention on how to achieve what you've set out to do.

That's one powerful method black belts use to blast past their fears. They focus on what they want.

Using the Outcome Frame

As you can see, the outcome frame changes your focus from developing problem statements to creating goal statements. This helps you see problems as challenges, opportunities to change, learn and grow.

This implies that "problems" are simply looking for a solution. They presuppose a desired outcome.

For example, when the new student asks "What if I cannot spar well and look really stupid?" they are really saying "My problem is that I am afraid of failure."

If you are struggling with this, you might ask yourself, "If you were not so afraid, what would you be feeling instead?"

This can lead you to an outcome statement like "to be confident so that I can enjoy and learn from my free sparring matches."

You can see these types of statements in all walks of life. A businessman may state a problem "sales are down." This assumes that their desired goal is to "increase sales."

By stating their outcome negatively people focus their attention back onto the problem. This forms an embedded suggestion in relation to the problem.

For example, the student who thinks "I don't want to be so afraid," is actually giving themselves the suggestion "be afraid".

The same goes for statements like: "I want to avoid embarrassment," "I want to quit smoking," "I want to lose weight," etc.

An outcome frame involves asking, "What do you want?"

This develops outcome statements such as "I want to enjoy myself" or "I want my lungs to be clear of smoke and tar" or "I want to be at the healthy weight of X".

That's the power of the outcome frame. It focuses your mind to follow a path that brings you to your desired state. It leads you towards a solution. It focuses you on what you want.

Now that you understand how to break past your fears you need to take action. That's what the next chapter is all about.

Chapter Five

Overcoming Inertia

"My great concern is not whether you have failed, but whether you are content with your failure." - **Abraham Lincoln**

The American Embassy in Australia offered his father a job when he was only 7 years old. His father took the job and left for the faraway country with his wife, leaving Kong-sang in Hong Kong to study.

His studies at the China Drama Academy were to prepare him for the Peking Opera and for the next ten years, he trained in acrobatics, singing, acting and martial arts. At seventeen he graduated from the Academy, but by then the Chinese Opera's popularity had faded. After a decade of specialized training, he couldn't find work in the opera anywhere.

Kong-sang could have taken the path of least resistance and gone to Australia to live with his parents. He could have blamed his inability to find work on bad luck and things outside of his control, but he didn't.

Instead, he took action. He looked for work and found it in the booming Hong Kong Kung Fu martial arts movies industry as a stuntman.

Being athletic, he could do every stunt asked of him. His amazing abilities impressed everyone in the industry. He soon found himself a much in demand stuntman in the new worldwide martial arts movie craze.

But just as quickly as it had risen, the demand for Kung Fu movies faded and all the stunt jobs dried up.

Unable to find any work at all, Kong-sang's parents encouraged him to move to Australia, and he finally did. He was working as a construction worker when he got a telegram from Willie Chan, a Hong Kong movie insider.

Kong-sang's stunt work had impressed Willie in "Fist of Fury" and he asked him to come back to Hong Kong to be in a follow-up, "New Fists of Fury". So, he returned to work in Hong Kong.

Even with this break, Kong-sang's career didn't take off. In fact, because the movies he was making didn't match his style, his first movies were unsuccessful. But he continued looking for ways to improve.

Eventually developed his own martial arts movie formula known as "Kung Fu comedy." He debuted this in the classic 1978 movie "Drunken Master". He followed that hit up with many other hit movies, including several American blockbusters.

Yes, Jackie Chan has clearly used most of his amazing abilities. As a result, has made a wonderful living doing what he loves, using movies to entertain us. But it all started when he decided to take action and found a job as a stuntman.

"When it is obvious that the goals cannot be reached, don't adjust the goals, adjust the action steps." - **Confucius**

Now that you've conquered your fears, you can't just think about becoming a black belt or writing the next blockbuster novel or starting your own business. No matter how hard you try to manifest something in your mind, until you take action, nothing happens.

James Malnichack is a wonderful speaking coach who is also a big MMA fan. In a talk I attended James told us, "To accomplish your goals you have to get off your assets."

James was telling us that if you want to accomplish anything, you can't just sit on the couch and think about it. You actually have to get up and do something.

Inertia

Newton's first law goes like this; "An object at rest stays at rest and an object in motion stays in motion with the same speed and in the same direction unless acted upon by an unbalanced force."

That's the problem with inertia. Watching martial arts movies can make becoming a black belt very appealing. But overcoming your inertia and getting off the couch and then walking into a martial arts gym can be very difficult.

Why? Because a body a rest tends to stay at rest.

Everyone runs into the problem of inertia. No matter how good your intentions are, if you don't take action, those intentions just don't matter. Without action, you don't achieve any traction. The result is your good intentions stay just that, good intentions that were never acted upon.

Action Blockers

Imagine a huge, round stone resting at the top of a hill held back by a tiny pebble at its base. If the tiny pebble was removed, the stone would begin to roll and, by the time it got to the bottom of the hill, it would roll over anything in its way.

That little stone is holding that stone back, keeping it from reaching the bottom. Just moving that little pebble would allow it to roll and gain the momentum it needs to roll to the bottom of the hill.

Just as the pebble keeps the stone from moving, the reason you don't move ahead is you're stuck. You are being held in place by inertia.

What's behind your inertia? The fear of failure and the fear of success.

What is the Fear of Failure

The fear of failure[6] was first studied in the 1960s when Stanford University psychologist John Atkinson tested children's motivation through a series of experiments.

The experiments he designed were simple but elegant, giving the children reward based tasks to determine their motivation.

The children's resulting behaviors divided them into two groups. One group approached the task with a "need for achievement" attitude. He found these children wanted to do better or achieve at a higher level.

The other group focused on their seemingly inevitable failure. This group's primary desire was to avoid the possibility of public humiliation because of their failure to accomplish the task. Atkinson named this phenomenon a "fear of failure".

In one experiment, Atkinson had the children play a game where they would toss a hoop over a peg from a measured distance. The rules gave a contestant more points the further they stood from the peg.

He found that children in the "need for achievement" group stood a challenging but realistic distance from the peg. If they failed to put the hoop around the peg, they would work on improving their technique or try to concentrate better.

Those who demonstrated the "fear of failure" phenomenon either stood right on top of the peg, so they could not fail, or were so far away from the peg that there was no way to succeed. When standing so close, it was, of course, impossible to fail.

But that left Atkinson with the question, "Why would some stand so far away?"

Atkinson's answer was that the ones who stood so far back were actually camouflaging their fear of failure. When attempting the task at an impossible distance, they could tell the other children that they hadn't failed due to lack of trying. They had tried their best and didn't succeed because they took greater risks.

They used this rationalization for themselves and for the other children. In their minds, had successfully disguised their fear of failure.

What's even more interesting is that many of the children who had demonstrated a fear of failure acted out and became disruptive. They said things like they didn't really want to play. Some even tried to stop the game.

Their fear of failure was much stronger than any reward they could possibly receive by trying and then being laughed at or humiliated when they failed.

Are You Being Held Back by the Fear of Failure?

"Fear will do one thing and one thing only: hold you back" -**Kya Aliana**

People who have a fear of failure will be reluctant to try something new and challenging.

This means a person could have the physical capability to become a black belt, but if they are afflicted with the fear of failure, they will never even try. They could have friends taking martial arts classes and hang on to every word they're told about the classes, but the fear of failure will, like the kids in the experiment, cause them to deny any interest in taking martial arts.

These are the ones that will say something like, "That stuff is fine for you. I just don't have time for all that training. Maybe I'll try it someday when I have more time."

Of course, more time never magically appears, and they never start training.

Or they might begin training but find themselves self-sabotaging, procrastinating going to class and then feigning disappointment when not allowed to take a belt test and then using that as an excuse to quit training.

They might say something like, "Well, I wanted to become a black belt but if they won't test me, I think I'll just quit" acting as if was the instructor's fault they couldn't make it to class.

Some have such low self-esteem or self-confidence that they never even try. They might, as many do, watch a martial arts demonstration and then say, "I'll never be good enough to do that," or "I'm not coordinated enough to kick like that."

Perfectionism

The big one that holds people back is perfectionism. These people attempt only those things they think they'll finish perfectly and successfully. Of course, this is a trap because, since no one is perfect, this plainly sets you up for failure.

While the entire purpose of martial arts training is perfection in body, mind and character, every martial artist understands that this is an unachievable goal. We motivate ourselves to perform at the highest level possible by striving for perfection.

Of course, the problem with accepting only perfection is you can do nothing perfectly. There is always room for improvement. This is especially true when trying something new.

People also wait for things to change, waiting for all conditions to be right. They are waiting for "the new job" or "to finish school" or whatever before they start. No one could ever become a black belt if they wait for all conditions to be perfect, to be right.

Waiting for conditions to be right is as insane as waiting for all the lights to be green before leaving for work in the morning! If you waited for all the lights to be green, you would never get on the road.

Lights are always changing on the way to work, just as conditions in your life are continuously changing. Conditions will never be right!

Perfectionism will hold you back from ever completing anything. You probably know people who have started a project and whenever you ask them about their project, they'll tell you "I still have a few bugs to work out but I'm still working on it" or "I'm still doing some edits on my book" (I know this one very well).

The perfectionist is the one who leaves the book unfinished, the song half done, the business plan on the drawing board, their dreams unfulfilled.

As John Greenleaf Whittier once said, "Of all sad words of tongue or pen, the saddest are these, 'it might have been.'".

Yes, the fear of failure manifests itself in many ways. It can hold you back if you let it, but it doesn't need to. The good news is if you've been experiencing the symptoms of the fear of failure, there are simple methods that a black belt uses that you can also use to deal with it, once and for all.

Using the Feedback vs. Failure Frame

"If you learn from defeat, you haven't really lost." - **Zig Ziglar**

How do you overcome this fear of failure? By changing how you view mistakes.

You overcome the failure frame by replacing it with the feedback frame.

Instead of focusing on failure, what you did "wrong", the feedback frame focuses your attention on how and what you can learn from a problem or mistake. This allows you to see mistakes and problems as learning experiences, as steppingstones to the right answer.

You use these events as feedback.

The Failure Mindset

Life is full of mistakes and setbacks. What determines whether you can overcome these setbacks is if you can see them as opportunities that bring you closer to your desired results, or only as failures that block you from ever achieving your goal.

When you don't get what you want, a failure mindset will bring up negative feelings, thoughts, and emotions about you and your abilities. As a result, you learn nothing useful from your actions. Instead, you reinforce the action that caused the mistake as you beat yourself up for "failing".

Since you are focused on the action that caused the mistake as you try to move toward your goals, your mind continuously brings up images of your "failure". This focus places obstacles on your path that are difficult, if not impossible, to overcome.

Life becomes a constant struggle. You become discouraged.

This mindset simply is not very useful.

The Feedback Mindset

When asked by a junior reporter, "How does it feel to have failed so many times to make a light bulb?" Thomas Edison replied, "I have not failed. I've just found 10,000 ways that won't work".

That's a perfect illustration of the feedback frame.

A feedback mindset steers your mind in a learning direction. It asks, "What did I learn?"

This frame focuses your mind on making the corrections you need to find the right solution, the solution that will allow you to achieve your desired outcome.

The feedback frame guides your thinking, helping you to understand that if what you are doing isn't working, it doesn't mean you have failed. What it means is you haven't yet achieved the results needed to bring you toward your goals.

Just as Thomas Edison pointed out, the feedback frame takes whatever results you get, no matter what happens, as feedback, ways that won't work. This feedback helps you uncover new solutions, solutions that bring you closer to the outcome you want.

Using the Feedback Frame

While sparring, a black belt is continually learning. If their opponent scores a point, they ask, "What technique did they just score with?" or "How did they set that technique up?" They might ask themselves, "What was I doing when that technique came in?" or "Where were my hands?" or "Was I distracted by something they did?"

They might even say something like, "Nice technique!" to their opponent and then make a mental note to figure out how they could use that same technique when sparring in the future.

The feedback frame allows them to maintain a more flexible attitude about sparring, using the feedback they receive as an opportunity to learn and improve. Instead of being bogged down by fear, the lessons they are learning motivate them. This frame allows them to relax, focus, and improve.

Black Belt Mind Secret # 6–Using Questions to Activate the Feedback Frame

The failure frame focuses on problems. When focused on problems, solutions remain hidden.

The feedback frame focuses on solutions. By focusing on the solution, you're a lot more likely to find one.

Here's how you can activate your feedback frame and start putting together the pieces of the puzzle facing you:

1. Write your failure thoughts.

To interrupt the failure frame, you need to recognize it as soon as it activates. This means when you find yourself thinking something like "That's a huge problem", or "I won't be able to do that" or "If I try this I'll probably fail and make a fool out of myself," you need to capture your thoughts on paper.

For example, maybe you are in a meeting or in a class and an answer comes to you, but at the same time, the thought" I'm afraid of being wrong" also pops into your mind.

Write that thought down!

Or perhaps you hear of a new opportunity at a startup company that fits your skills perfectly but then you think "What happens if I (or the company) fail, and I end up in a worse place than where I started?" Write that thought down!

2. Develop feedback frame questions.

As we discussed before, feedback frame questions are those that focus your mind on solutions. While the questions you might ask are endless, the following are a few examples that you may find useful:

When things go wrong:

Things rarely go the way we would like them to. When this happens, instead of asking "Why does this always happen to me?" ask, "What's good about this?" Now write your response.

If you can't think of anything good about what has happened, ask yourself, "What could be good about this?" and write your response.

When you make a mistake:

No matter how good we are, there will always be times when we make a mistake or two. Let's say you are late for an important meeting. Instead of asking "Why am I always late, ask, "What can I do to be on time in the future?"

Realize that mistakes are simply a part of being human. The question, "What could I do differently in the future so this won't happen again?" helps focus your mind on getting the feedback you need that allows you to make corrections.

When you are afraid of making a mistake:

Let's say your company offered you a new position, but you're afraid that you won't be able to do the job perfectly. You're afraid that this might make you seem foolish.

Instead of saying "I could never do that" or "What happens if I mess this up?" ask "What's the worst thing that could happen if I do this?"

You might think, "People would think less of me or think that I'm incompetent" or "I could get fired!" Write all the answers you come up with.

Now ask "Can I live with that result?"

Unless what you are planning to do could kill you or land you in jail, the honest answer is almost always "yes".

After you answer "yes" to the "can I live with this?" question, you can now focus your mind in a more positive direction by asking "What's the best thing that could happen if I do this?" Now write your response.

By using questions to focus on the feedback you're receiving, you are training your mind to search for a path to success. Now instead of thinking about failure, you are thinking you just haven't found the way yet. That's a true black belt mind secret.

The Fear of Success

The fear of success[7] was first examined by psychologist Matina Horner in the early 1970s. This fear can be just as big, or even bigger, a barrier to success than the fear of failure.

You might think, "Who would be afraid of success? Doesn't everyone want to be successful?"

On the surface, nearly everyone would agree with you. People are driven to succeed, aren't they? The unfortunate truth is sometimes this isn't the case.

Some people fear what success might bring them. The fear of success is a kind of mirror image of the fear of failure. Only instead of humiliation, you fear success because you are afraid of rejection.

Why Would Someone Equate Success with Rejection?

The rejection you fear comes from being afraid that the people around you will judge you negatively and eventually leave you. The facts are that change makes people uncomfortable. Nobody really likes to change. They might tolerate it, but they really don't like it.

As you move along the path toward success, your journey will alter who you are. It will make you look at your world and the people in it differently.

The people in your life realize this and, as a result, they aren't as excited about your change as you are. In fact, as you work on your success, you'll probably have more to do and your friends might make comments like, "You don't have time for us anymore" or "You seem like you're working all the time" or something else to "guilt you out" about your success.

They might make comments similar to the old Midwestern saying that says you are "Getting too big for your britches," implying that the reason your relationship isn't the same is because you are getting too "uppity".

Your success is changing you and they don't like that!

The real problem is they don't want to do the things they need to do to become a more successful person. They don't want to change, so they try to pull you down.

Don't Let the Crabs of Failure Pull You Down

Before we go on, I want to tell you a story I heard a long time ago about fishing for crabs.

Anyone who has ever gone "crabbing" knows that in order to catch crabs, you need three things: a crab cage, a rope and some bait.

The crab cage is just a rectangular looking wire-framed box, about 24 inches by 18 inches, with an opening at the top that has a door opening similar to a birdcage. This opening allows crabs to crawl into the cage.

Catching the crabs is fairly easy. Put the bait (fish heads and other such items) into the crab cage and lower it down to the bottom or the ocean floor with a rope. Now wait.

What will happen is crabs will notice the bait and figure out how to crawl in. They climb to the top, float down to the bottom, and start feasting on the tasty fish heads.

Other crabs will notice the crab feast and they too will crawl into the cage. More and more crabs will crawl in and feast on fish heads until the food is gone.

About that time, one crab will think, "There's no food. I should leave" and try to crawl out of the cage. The problem is that the other crabs don't want them to leave and will pull them back down. In fact, if the crab tries too hard to get out of the cage, the other crabs will pull it apart and have another crab feast!

Sometimes friends can act like those crabs.

They don't want you to pull yourself out of the cage that you're in.

They don't want you to grow. They try to pull you back down.

These people are not your friends.

They are simply people who are envious of your desire and motivation to improve and don't want to put in the work necessary for their own success.

You Can Only Change Yourself

As you train in the martial arts, you'll make training buddies. Every day as you go to class, you will look for these training buddies, ask them how their training is going. You learn about their aspirations and goals inside and outside of the martial arts.

You might get to know them very well, hanging out with them outside of class as well. You become more than training buddies, you become friends. Some of these friendships last a lifetime.

Then, one day, your friend will not come to class. Then they'll miss a few classes in a row.

Finally, you call them and ask what's going on. While there could be some kind of emergency, some kind of crisis or some medical reason, usually what happens is your friend just doesn't want to put in the effort anymore. Training in martial arts is no longer a priority for them.

You keep in touch, even going out for coffee or to lunch every once in a while. You tell them about people you both trained with, but they aren't really that interested. When you talk with them, you can tell that they're just not that interested in your training.

They might even suggest that training "takes too much time" and suggest that you do something with them that doesn't involve the martial arts, something that they know will take time away from your goal. You politely decline, gently pointing out the conflict.

Soon you're seeing less and less of your friend, but you continue to train. Finally, one day you're ready to take a test for your black belt. You invite your friend to watch. They politely (or maybe not so politely) decline your invitation.

They don't come because they don't want to see you succeed. They are secretly, and not so secretly, jealous of your success. They know that they had the same opportunity that you did, but they decided not to put in the effort needed to earn their black belt.

This might make you a little sad. You wanted them to earn their black belt at the same time as you. But you can't make someone else succeed. You can only give them the tools they need in order to better themselves and the guidance to use those tools. The rest is up to them.

If they decide not to use those tools, if they decide not to change, it's not on you, it's on them.

A central fact you learn early in psychology classes is you can't change other people or other things. You can only change yourself. No matter how much you try, no matter how much you want it for them, unless a person wants to change their life, they never will.

The problem is as you begin to succeed, they often want to pull you back down to their level. They want you stuck in the same cage that they are.

To stay on course, you need to keep taking action. How can you motivate yourself to take action? You inspire yourself to take action using the outcome frame.

Reviewing the Outcome Frame

When flying on a plane, why do the flight attendants tell passengers that in an emergency, when the oxygen masks come down from the overhead to place it over their mouth and nose first even before their children?

It's because if you don't place it over your mouth and nose first, there's a good chance you'll pass out and your children can't help you. Now you have a wideawake, helpless child that is in danger of losing oxygen.

Not a good scenario.

When you have friends that are struggling, the best thing you can do is to succeed. By succeeding, you can blaze the path and they can follow in your footsteps.

If you fear success because of what your friends might think, you are picturing success as a problem.

This might lead you to ask yourself disempowering questions like, "Why does my friend keep ignoring me? Is it because they think I'm trying too hard to improve myself?" or "What happens if I achieve my goals and my friends don't like me anymore?"

If you want to help give your friends a chance to succeed, instead of allowing your mind to roam wild on the negative side, you need to change your focus by using the outcome frame to find a solution.

For example, when you ask "Why does my friend keep ignoring me? Is it because they think I'm trying too hard to improve myself?" you are really saying "I'm afraid my friends think I'm trying to get rid of them. They think I want to throw them away."

Instead, you might ask yourself, "What would I like my friends to think?"

This can lead you to an outcome statement like "I want my friends to be happy for my success and see that if I can do it so can they."

But what happens if your friend continues to try to pull you back into the cage? How can you use outcome statements to continue to take action even in the face of losing a friendship?

Again, ask yourself an outcome question such as, "What is my most important value here? Is it my friendship with a friend who doesn't seem to want to grow with me right now, or is it my personal growth and success?"

Your answer will most likely be, "I want to grow and be personally successful."

Now your next question needs to be, "What do I need to do in order to stay focused on growing and becoming successful?"

Once you've trained your mind to focus on outcomes, your conscious and subconscious minds will begin to work together to help you find the right solution.

This might be, "I will still love my friend and wish the best for them, but I choose to stay focused on becoming the person I need to be to achieve the success I desire."

Notice that you have not "thrown away" your friend. You have left the door open for them to come back into your life anytime they want. What you have done is decide to concentrate on the one thing you can control: yourself.

That's how you break past the fears that hold you back, that keep you from getting started. But in order to do that, you need to be driven into taking action by the outcome you desire.

You need to create a burning desire.

Chapter Six

Developing a Burning Desire

"Should you desire the great tranquility, prepare to sweat." -
Hakuin

She was a pretty teenage girl. She had been born the year after World War II and had ended up in Shanghai, where she lived with her family. Then, when she was only 15, her world crumbled as she and her younger sister were abandoned. Her parents left them to fend for themselves.

She had been trained as a ballet dancer but could only find work playing male characters in Chinese Opera films. To keep food on the table and a roof over their heads, she threw herself into her work, playing her parts the very best she knew how.

By chance, a young Chinese director saw her and thought she would be perfect for a starring role in a movie he was making for the new Wu Xia (Swordsman) films that were taking the Hong Kong movie market by storm. She was sensational and her part in the 1965 movie "Come Drink With Me" became the inspiration Ang Lee used to model the Oscar-winning "Crouching Tiger, Hidden Dragon".

Since her humble beginning, Cheng Pei has made over sixty movies including playing the character Jade Fox in Ang Lee's "Crouching Tiger, Hidden Dragon". She did all that not because of her aspiration to become a brilliant actress, but out of necessity. Cheng Pei Pei became the first "Queen of Kung Fu Films" out of a burning desire to provide for herself and her sister.

When Do You Really Want to Succeed?

If you read or watch biographies of people who have succeeded at a high level, a common thread is they had a burning desire to be successful. While sometimes circumstances, like those that happened to Cheng Pei Pei, motivate them to act, more often it's when external and internal forces merge at just the right time in just the place that motivates a person to take action.

It's like the story about an old wise and successful martial arts teacher who lived in a beautiful house close to the sea. He had practiced martial arts for many decades and because of his fame, was living a very comfortable life.

He was a man of letters and had studied many subjects, mastering them all. It was said that he was so wise that had mastered life itself and could answer any question anyone might ask him.

One day, a young black belt from far away visited the wise old master. He traveled for many days before finally arriving at the old man's home.

The young black belt climbed the steps to the house and rapped on the door. The sun was just beginning to set as the old master swung the door open, smiled and said, "Hello! What can I do for you?"

The young black belt bowed respectfully and told the master, "I have a question I'd like to ask you."

The old master smiled broadly and replied, "Young man, it looks like you've traveled a long way to visit me."

The young black belt nodded and said, "Yes, sir, I have. From the other side of the country"

"Then come inside and we'll talk."

As the young black belt stepped through the door, the old master asked, "Are you hungry?"

"Yes, sir."

"Then have dinner with me," the old man said, still beaming.

The young black belt started to protest when the wise master frowned slightly. Raising his hand, he sternly told the young black belt, "I insist."

While cooking dinner, the old man made small talk. After they were through eating, he asked, "What is the question you traveled so far to ask me?"

The young man smiled and said, "Sir, I want to know how to be as wise and successful as you."

For a long while, the old master rubbed his chin as he gazed at the young man, seemingly trying to come up with an answer.

Finally, with a very sincere look, he said, "This is a very complex question. You've traveled a long way and must be tired. Why don't you get some rest now? I'll wake you after I've given your question some more thought. You can sleep in the room in the back of the house."

Again, the young black belt started to protest. Again, the wise old master frowned slightly and said, "I insist."

The young black belt nodded and then bowed to the old man before retiring to his room. He was exhausted, and the bed was wonderfully soft. Within minutes he had fallen sound asleep.

That morning at 5 AM the old man burst into the young man's room shouting, "Get dressed! I have your answer!"

The young black belt jumped out of bed, dressed quickly and met the old man who was waiting outside his room.

The old man led him outside into the moonlit night and down to the edge of the ocean. "Take off your shoes" he said "and follow me" as he stepped into the pre-dawn surf.

The young black belt kicked off his shoes, thinking, "Is this old man crazy?" but followed the old master into the surf, anyway.

The water became deeper and deeper, up to his knees, then up to his waist and finally just below his chest. The sun was just beginning to creep into the sky and he could see the old master just ahead, motioning for him to follow until the water was at his neck.

"What's this about?" the young black belt shouted over the sound of the waves. "How does this answer my question?"

Just as the last syllable left the young black belt's lips, the old man grabbed his head and pushed it under the water. The young black belt started to panic, thinking that the old man WAS crazy. Fiercely, he struggled to free himself from the old man's grasp. But the old man easily clasped his head under the surf.

By now he thought that the old man was simply going to kill him and, as he began to pass out, just as suddenly as the old man had grabbed his head and pushed it under water, he jerked the young black belt's head up out of the water.

As he walked back toward the shore, he shouted, "Follow me!"

When they got to the shore, the young black belt looked warily at the old master. Keeping his distance, he shouted, "What was that all about?"

Softy, the old man answered, "What was the one thing you wanted more than anything else before I pulled your head out of the water?"

"To breathe!" the young black belt exclaimed.

"Ah, when you want to succeed as much as you wanted to breathe just now, then you will be successful." Then the old master strolled back up the beach toward his house under the slowly rising sun.

That's the secret of success. To desire it so much that it is more important than any other thing in your life. To have the same burning desire and determination to succeed as you would if your head was stuck under water and you needed to get some air.

What is a Burning Desire?

"I have a dream." - **Dr. Martin Luther King Jr.**

Dr. King had a dream "that my four little children will one day live in a nation where they will not be judged by the color of their skin but by the content of their character."

He had a big dream, and it is coming to fruition. More than ever, people are being judged by the content of their character instead of the color of their skin. As proof, as I write this, our first mixed race president, President Obama, sits in the White House.

Everyone who has achieved anything at a high level has achieved their success because they had a big dream, a burning desire.

For some, like Steve Jobs, it was to find creative ways to use technology. For others, like Jonas Salk, it is to solve a medical puzzle, developing a cure for polio. Some, like Bruce Lee, it was to bring part of his culture onto the world screen.

No matter what their desire, what these people had in common was a vision of what they wanted to achieve. We'll discuss how to develop that vision a little later. Right now, let's start by developing a declaration of what you desire.

What is a Desire Declaration?

"We hold these truths to be self-evident, that all men are created equal, that they are endowed by their Creator with certain unalienable rights that among these are Life, Liberty and the pursuit of Happiness." - **The Declaration of Independence**

The men who wrote the words above were big dreamers, declaring what they wanted their world, and the world of their children and children's children, to be like. These powerful words created a powerful, burning desire in those early Americans that enabled them to become independent of the greatest power in the world at the time.

In order for you to achieve whatever you want, you need to be able to develop that same burning desire. You can do it the same way those early Americans did, by creating a powerful desire declaration.

Write it Down!

"Until you write it down it's just a dream." - **Unknown**

If you want to accomplish something great you need to write it down.

By writing it down, you are creating a map, a path to follow. A map makes it a lot easier to get to where you want to go.

By having a map, you are creating a destination, somewhere where you want to end up.

Also, by writing out your desire declaration, you are committing to its accomplishment. You are making a promise to yourself.

That's the reason most people never write down anything they want to accomplish. They're too timid to commit to its accomplishment.

Carry Your Goals Around with You

In the classic self-help book, 'Think and Grow Rich", Napoleon Hill[8] talks about writing your goals and carrying them around in your wallet. That was back in 1937. Since then, every self-help author and motivational speaker has stressed the importance of writing your goals.

What's interesting is that very few people do this, but those that do often go on to accomplish incredible things.

You can see a great example of this in a 1997 interview with Oprah (you can find it on YouTube). Jim Carrey talks about writing his goal in an interesting and unique way in this interview. In 1991, when he was flat broke, he wrote himself a $10 million check, dating it 'Thanksgiving 1995'. In the notation area, he wrote 'For acting services rendered.'

He put the check in his wallet and visualized its achievement as he drove from audition to audition, getting turned down time after time. Then in 1994, he received $10 million for his role in the movie "Dumb and Dumber".

Although it wasn't a traditional way of writing a goal, that's in essence what Jim Carrey did. He combined his declaration with hard work and creative visualization, which we'll talk about a little later, and achieved it.

Think Big

"Think little goals and expect little achievements. Think big goals and win big success." - **David Joseph Schwartz - The Magic of Thinking Big**

High achievers also tell you to think big. Big dreams will spur you on to take massive action. Massive action will get you massive results.

One of the most interesting stories I ever heard about taking massive action was told by the motivational speaker, Anthony Robbins[9]. Early in his career they invited him to the former Soviet Union along with a few other people working in the personal/brain development field to discuss their findings with Soviet scientists.

On his trip, Tony wrote all his goals for the next five years. They were huge, massive goals, making $1 million a year, buying a house, getting married. His goals were enormous. What was fascinating about his story is they all came true–the next year!

But he didn't just think big, he took massive action. As any successful person will tell you, it takes massive action to get massive results.

Make it Specific!

"You cannot make it as a wandering generality. You must become a meaningful specific." - **Zig Ziglar**

You can't hit what you can't see. To achieve the success you desire, your desire has to be laser focused. It has to be something specific, not, as Zig Ziglar put it, a wandering generality, something vague or general.

A long time ago, I read a story about Howard Hill who was the greatest archer of his time. Because of the bows and arrows he used, some consider him the greatest archer of all time.

Howard Hill was so accurate and effective that he killed bull elephants, Bengal Tigers, African Lions and Cape buffalo with only a bow and arrow. Not only was he an amazing archer, he also had nerves of steel.

It was said that at 50 feet, Howard Hill could out-shoot any rifleman in the world. He could hit the center of the target and then split his previous arrow with his following shot.

But if Howard Hill was alive today, I know I could out-shoot him every time. That is, if you let me blindfold him and spin him around a few dozen times before allowing him to pull back on his bow. Not only would he be effectively blind, but he would be dizzy and unable to locate the direction of the target.

Now you might think "that's not fair" and you'd be right. But that's what happens when you can't "see" your target, when it's a wandering generality.

You need to identify your target specifically, or you'll never hit anything. Your mind must be laser focused on your goal.

The drive you need to take massive action comes from having specific desire.

Now let's get started on Black Belt Mind Secret # 7 - Creating Your Desire Declaration

Alright, it's time to build your burning desire. The first part is to declare what you want. Use the following three steps to create your desire declaration.

Step One - Write 5 Positive Beliefs

To get your desired declarations started in the right direction, write five positive beliefs you have about yourself.

This might be something like "I persistently go after my goals no matter the obstacles" or "I've can quickly solve complex problems" or "My body is strong and flexible."

These belief statements should be short, quick thoughts you feel strongly about. You might even write something as short as "I'm smart in math" or "I can run a mile in less than 7 minutes".

Write your five positive beliefs:

_____
_____
_____
_____
_____
_____
_____

Before you go on, read these belief statements out loud with emotion, feeling, and conviction. The best way to do this is in front of a mirror.

As you read them, if you find that you're unsure of them, go through the belief building exercise in Black Belt Mind Secret #2.

Back to Beliefs

William James once said, "Believe that life is worth living and your belief will help create the fact."

All significant accomplishments start with belief. Your desire declaration needs to be congruent with who you are. It needs to be something you believe you can accomplish.

As you begin, ask yourself, "Do I believe I can accomplish this?" If the answer is "no" then go through the belief building process found earlier in this book.

As you go through the belief building exercise, remember the wise words of Gail Devers: "Understand to achieve anything requires faith and belief in yourself, vision, hard work, determination, and dedication. Remember all things are possible for those who believe."

Doing this process prepares your mind, just as the farmer prepares the soil, for the seeds of greatness you are about to plant in your mind.

Desire Declaration Step 2 – Write Your Desire Declaration

Now it's time to write your desire declaration. Remember to make your desire declaration big and specific.

If your desire declaration is around getting into better physical shape, instead of writing something as simple and sweet like, "I am in good physical shape," write something specific such as

"I am healthy, trim and fit. I weigh 164 pounds and I am in the top 3 percent fitness level of all people."

If your desire declaration is around making more money instead of writing "to be rich" your desire statement would be something like "I am earning $250,000 a year and am investing 20 percent of the money I earn. This gives me over $1 million in investments in seven years."

Now write out your desire declaration. Remember – Think Big!

_____
_____
_____
_____
_____
_____
_____
_____

Desire Declaration Step 3–Commit to Your Desire Declaration

"Our life always expresses the result of our dominant thoughts."
- Soren Kierkegaard

Your desire declaration is the map to the future you desire. This map gives you the plan to get to where you want to go.

While maps can make life easier, the best maps are the ones you can access without opening a book or looking at a GPS, like the one that brings you home every day, one that's a well-worn path.

To be useful, your desire statement needs to be assessable, on the tip of your tongue at all times. Something you can access without opening your notebook or looking at your computer.

You can make your desire statement a well-worn path by writing it in a notebook or journal every morning and every evening and then repeating it out loud. As you do this, read it with belief, enthusiasm, purpose and conviction.

As it becomes a dominant thought, your mind starts to commit to it, doing whatever it takes to accomplish what you've set out to do. This is how you light the fire of your burning desire.

Now let's look at how to turn this flame into such a furious fire that nothing can stand in its way.

Chapter Seven

Self-Direction

"I fear not the man who has practiced 10,000 kicks once, but I fear the man who has practiced one kick 10,000 times." - **Bruce Lee**

When he was only two years old, Li Lianjie's father died. His family, like most that go through this type of tragedy, struggled to make ends meet.

When he was eight years old, they discover his talent for Wushu. He then began training with Li Junfeng and Wu Bin, the most famous Wushu coaches in China. Li Lianjie threw himself into his training and within three years, he had won his first national championship and a gold medal for the Beijing Wushu Team.

By the time he was 19, he had won sixteen gold and one silver medal, defeating mostly adults.

His fame as a national champion opened doors for an acting career and Li Lianjie focused on combining great acting with excellent martial arts, moving the martial arts movie industry to a new level of entertainment.

Today, Li Lianjie is a household name. Only most people know him by his English stage name, Jet Li, but he would have never got there without the self-discipline needed to pursue his goals persistently.

Dedicated Effort

"We all have dreams. But in order to make dreams come into reality, it takes an awful lot of determination, dedication, self-discipline, and effort." - **Jessie Owens**

There's a story about a world-renowned pianist who was walking down 56th street in Manhattan one afternoon, relaxing before his concert that evening. A stranger approached him and said, "May I ask you a question?"

"Of course," he answered, smiling, thinking that they would ask him for an autograph.

"How do you get to Carnegie Hall?"

The pianist frowned slightly. After a moment, he loudly muttered, "Practice, practice, practice," and then walked away.

The pianist was simply stating the obvious. In order to accomplish anything in life, you need to have more than talent. You need to put in the hours of practice needed to hone your craft.

You need to know the direction you're going and then take consistent action toward your destination. Success requires self-discipline.

Self-Discipline

People who succeed take disciplined action. It is the key to all success.

The people that take disciplined action become black belts, finish college, write books, compete in the Olympics, become research scientists or whatever success means to that person. Self-discipline is what drives you to take the action you need to do in order to complete the tasks that lead to success.

There are people who have the natural abilities; the intelligence, the physical talent, and coordination, whatever they needed for success but never "reach their potential". These are the ones who lack this vital ingredient.

These naturally talented individuals don't rise to the top because they don't run that extra lap, study that extra hour, write that one more page or practice that form one more time.

How Self-Discipline Trumps Talent

I went to college at the University of San Diego. During my studies there, I met several extraordinary people. One of my classmates, Mari Carmen Casta, was a tennis player who eventually became a highly ranked professional.

A few years after we graduated, Mari Carmen decided to get married. She invited me to her wedding and seated me beside her college tennis coach, Scott McCarthy, at her reception.

By that time, I had my own martial arts school, and I was curious about his perspective, so I asked him about coaching and what ages he enjoyed coaching the most.

Scott told me, "I enjoy teaching kids. In the summer, I get the opportunity to coach them and see them grow."

Then I asked, "How do you know which ones are talented enough to play at a high level? Which ones succeed?"

Scott thought for a moment and then said, "I see a lot of kids who have a lot of talent and when they start, they beat everyone. As a result, they don't practice; they just rely on their talent to win."

"On the other hand, kids will come in without as much 'natural' talent and, because the ones with the 'natural' talent constantly beat them, they practice, and practice, and practice."

After six months or so, the not so talented kids are beating the very' talented' ones and the 'talented' ones quit. They get discouraged when they can't win on just talent anymore."

Scott's observation was that the ones who were less 'talented' excelled because they desired to get better. This motivated them to practice.

Their desire, coupled with practice, helped them to develop the habits of success. Using disciplined action, they were able to succeed.

The Music of the Martial Arts

If you ask a black belt what the number one characteristic of any black belt is, some may say persistence, some may say determination but, with a little prodding, all of them will agree that in order to become a black belt you need a boatload of self-discipline.

Learning martial arts is like learning to play a musical instrument. You go to music class to learn how to play the instrument. After teaching you the basics, your teacher shows you new ways to perform and gives you new songs and melodies.

For learning how to play your instrument, your time with your teacher is invaluable. But no matter how good your teacher is, without practice, your techniques won't improve.

Practice makes you able to perform fluidly and (hopefully) flawlessly. Practice turns the musician's mechanical skills of moving their finger over a mechanical device into an incomparably beautiful experience that can enrapture nearly everyone who hears their music.

Musicians who play at this level are in a world of their own, playing nearly without thinking.

To learn a martial art, you go through the same process. You attend classes with your instructor to learn the basics. After learning the basics, you learn how to combine them. With time, your balance and coordination improve, along with your flexibility and stamina. This allows you to learn more advanced techniques.

But you can only learn new techniques after you have a firm grasp of the more basic ones. This only comes with practice.

While you can practice your techniques at your martial arts school, in order to perform those techniques at a top level, you need to practice them on your own.

Practicing what you are learning is what raises your level of expertise.

This takes self-discipline because the only way this can ever become a reality is to practice when you're tired or when you would rather go with your friends to the mall. You make yourself practice no matter what other interesting things might be going on.

You practice because you have a goal, an outcome you have committed to.

So, self-discipline is what "makes" a black belt. To become a black belt, you must take disciplined action, practicing when it's uncomfortable, when it's hard, when you don't want to.

You must make a habit of practice.

Habits

"All our life so far as it is has definite form, is but a mass of habits–practical, emotional and intellectual–systematically organized for our weal or woe, and bearing us irresistibly toward our destiny, whatever that latter might be." - **William James**

According to Dictionary.com, we can define a habit as "an acquired behavior pattern regularly followed until it has become almost involuntary."

In the United States, most people have the habit of brushing their teeth in the morning. What's interesting is that until about 100 years ago, this wasn't the case. Before that time, the majority of people didn't brush their teeth at all.

Today in the United States, we think of the habit of brushing one's teeth as an important habit, something that everyone should do. In fact, someone who hasn't gained this habit will be very unpopular with the people they encounter.

In this case, brushing your teeth is a habit because it is a social norm, something that we expect everyone to do. When society expects us to do something, most people conform.

If you don't conform, there can be, and usually are, sanctions.

That's why, for most people, these types of social norms are easy habits to maintain. Most people conform because not to conform to a social norm can mean being disliked and ignored at the least. At worst, not following a social norm can lead to scorn and rejection by the group as a whole.

Other habits may or may not be so easy to obtain.

For example, exercising daily takes discipline. That is, unless you have made exercise a habit. Then exercising is easy.

If exercising is a habit and you regularly go to the gym every Monday, Wednesday, and Friday after work, you might find yourself steering your car in the direction of the gym. This will happen even if you've made plans to see a movie with a friend at your regular workout time.

The bad thing is that good habits are easy to lose. Even if going to the gym has become a habit for you, if you stop going for a few weeks, it can be a tough habit to start up again.

This is because of the effort it takes to set this habit in motion again.

On the other hand, a habit like smoking cigarettes can be easy to start but hard to get rid of. If you smoke, or know someone who does, then you also know that giving up smoking can be an arduous process.

Why? It's the same reason it's hard to start going to the gym–it takes effort to quit smoking.

Black belts understand this about habits. So, they continue to train regularly. Because if they don't, they know they will lose their habit.

But how did they form this habit to begin with?

Forming New Habits

Here's how a habit works at a very basic level.

You experience a cue or trigger. The cue is associated with a reward. To receive the reward, you need to do a routine. So, your brain develops the following pattern.

Cue -> Routine -> Reward

Let's say you have a habit of eating a candy bar every day at three o'clock in the afternoon. To make things simple, let's say your cue is looking at the clock at seeing the time, three o'clock.

Again, for simplicity's sake, let's say your reward is the energy rush you get from the sugar in the cookie. You have learned that when you eat the cookie; you get a nice little rush. That's your reward.

Here's what your habit looks like:

Three o'clock -> Eat Cookie -> Energy Rush

To change this habit, you need to keep your cue. You also need to keep your reward. But you need to change your routine.

How?

You need to give your brain an energy rush differently.

Let's say you replace eating a cookie at three o'clock for a quick, 10-minute walk around the building. You are on the third floor, so you go down one flight of stairs and up another. At the end of the walk, you get a nice little energy rush.

Let's look at your new habit:

Three o'clock -> Take a Walk -> Energy Rush

Since your brain doesn't know the difference between the energy you get from sugar and the energy you get from increasing your endorphins by walking, you trick your brain into associating walking with the reward you crave.

Presto! You have established a new habit!

Well, maybe not.

Repetition–the Real Habit Maker

Habits, even the worst ones, don't happen because of having a onetime experience.

For example, heroin addicts don't become addicted after one exposure to heroin (although it can make them more susceptible). The facts are that while there are people who develop pathological dependence ("addiction") to heroin, most people (75-85%) can use heroin for a while and stop using when they decide to stop.

Studies find that there are very complex reasons for heroin addiction, including repeated exposure (repetition).

The same goes for cigarette smoking or overeating. Just because you smoke one cigarette doesn't make you addicted to nicotine. Nor does one instance of gorging yourself on Thanksgiving suddenly cause you to overeat constantly.

These types of behaviors become habits after repeated exposure. Repetition develops habit.

The same goes for good habits.

Someone who habitually trains in the martial arts doesn't start that way. They had to expose themselves to classes repeatedly before having the routine of grabbing their gear and getting into their car after they saw it was six o'clock (their cue).

So why do some people develop good habits and others don't?

Back to Beliefs

"Belief creates the actual fact." - **William James**

To gain a new habit or to exchange one habit for another, you need to believe that you can make that change. You need to shift your beliefs.

Remember, a belief it is just a memory. It isn't necessarily right or wrong, it just is.

William James came from a very successful and prosperous family. Both his brother Henry and his father Henry Sr. were very accomplished in their fields.

William started out life as a sickly child and then wandered about into his thirties trying to "find himself". He started out as an artist, actually a painter. A while later, he attended medical school. Then he dropped out to explore the Amazon River.

After all this self-exploration, William could not find the sense in it all and became depressed. When he was 28 years old, he wrote, "Today I touched bottom, and perceive plainly that I must face the choice with open eyes. Shall I frankly throw the moral business overboard, as one unsuited to my innate inaptitude?"

This seems to imply that William James was contemplating ending his life. He began believing that suicide would be his best course of action. Then, for some unknown reason, he decided to put off his decision.

Two months later, he made a different decision. He decided to try a yearlong experiment where he would spend twelve months believing that he could become better.

During this time, he would believe that he was in control and that his free will would help him change his destiny. In his diary he wrote, "I will assume for the present–until next year–that it is no illusion. My first act of free will shall be to believe in free will."

Then he went to work to strengthen this belief.

His work led him to become a professor at Harvard University, a respected lecturer, the father of American psychology and a well-respected philosopher. These accomplishments resulted from his taking repeated action every day.

His repeated actions created his new beliefs. This changed his life.

Repeated Action

So why do some people take repeated action and move toward their goals while others don't?

It's because they haven't incorporated their "why" into their daily routine. It's your "why" that will get you to take action when it's hard.

The best way to do is to create "Top of Mind" awareness of your "why". In marketing, top-of-mind awareness is "a brand or specific product coming first in customers' minds when thinking of a particular industry." It's the product you think of first when you go shopping.

For example, what's your favorite brand of toothpaste?

If you have a favorite brand when you go shopping, you don't think about which box to reach for, you just reach for your favorite brand.

How did you go about choosing this as your favorite brand of toothpaste? There's a very good chance that you "chose" this brand because of being exposed to media exposure. Companies use channels such as the Internet, radio, newspapers, television, magazines, and social media to help you choose and, as a result, your choice happens automatically, without thinking.

You can use a similar technique to create "Top of Mind" awareness for your "why".

Affirmations

"It's the repetition of affirmations that leads to belief. And once that belief becomes a deep conviction, things begin to happen." - **Muhammad Ali**

The simplest way to create "Top of Mind" awareness for your "why" is to use affirmations that focus your mind on the goal you are trying to achieve.

For an affirmation to be affective it needs to involve the 4 "P's". These are:

1) Your affirmation needs to be "positive".

Your affirmation must be what you want rather than what you don't want.

You've decided to take martial arts classes because martial arts have always intrigued you, but you've always had one excuse or another not to take classes. The reason you want to take martial arts classes is because you're about 20 pounds heavier than you'd like to be.

You decide to develop an affirmation that will inspire you to get into the shape you'd like to be.

You could go about this a couple of ways. The first is creating the affirmation "I am going to lose 20 pounds."

This affirmation has a couple of problems, but let's deal only with the aspect of it not being positive. This affirmation is negative because nobody likes to lose anything, not even 20 pounds. So, this affirmation focuses on what you don't want.

Instead, focus your affirmation on what you'll gain. You could do this by saying, "My healthy eating and exercise habits allow me to gain my ideal body weight goal."

2) Your affirmation needs to be stated in the present tense.

State your goal as if you had already accomplished it. Affirmation in the present tense, you engage your imagination in the attraction mode. This helps to pull your goals toward you.

In the example above, we talked about creating the affirmation "I am going to lose 20 pounds."

Not only did this affirmation focus on what you don't want, you also stated it in the future. So does the affirmation "My healthy eating and exercise habits allow me to gain my ideal body weight goal."

Let's tweak this second affirmation and say, "because of my healthy eating and exercise habits, I weigh (fill in the amount). I am healthy, trim and fit!"

You now have a positive, present tense affirmation that links your goal to what you're willing to do to achieve it.

3) Your affirmation needs to be personal.

An affirmation can never be about the behavior of anyone else. It needs to be about you. You have no control over other people or things. You only have control over yourself.

Perhaps you're having issues with your relationship, and you make the affirmation "My (husband/wife girlfriend/boyfriend) is pleased with my efforts to relate better with (him/her).

Even though you are affirming the work you're willing to do, my efforts to relate better with (him/her), this is not a personal affirmation. You cannot affect how your significant other reacts to your charming efforts to please them.

You can, however, with a small shift you can focus your affirmation completely on your behavior, saying "I am spending a minimum of 30 minutes every evening communicating with my (husband/wife girlfriend/boyfriend). I listen to what (he/she) has to say and share my thoughts and feelings with (him/her).

All of this is under your control.

What most people find is that by making a shift in their behavior, they notice a shift in other people's behavior. While this isn't always the case, it is the case most of the time.

Focus your affirmation on what you can do, and the results will follow. If you don't get the results you want, use it as feedback and change your approach, again focusing on what you can do.

4) When saying your affirmation, you need to involve your physiology.

You've decided you want to earn your black belt. You feel it's worth the sacrifice and effort.

Just saying an affirmation such as "I have earned my black belt by going to class three days a week and working out on my own three days a week" is helpful.

But when you involve your physiology, you put your affirmation on steroids.

What do I mean by involving your physiology?

Walk around the room pumping your fists into the air while repeating your affirmation out loud. This activates all your representational systems, visual, auditory and kinesthetic.

This, in turn, helps motivate you to take the action you need to achieve the goal you desire.

Black Belt Mind Secret #8 - Practicing Daily Affirmations

Black Belt Mind Secret #8 helps you get the most out of your affirmations, using them to motivate yourself to take the action you need. It moves you from the mindset of," I have to (whatever it is you need to do)," to "I can't wait to get started!"

Use these steps to get the most out of your affirmations:

1) Create affirmations that motivate you.

There are many ways of creating daily affirmations.

I believe the best affirmations are the ones you personally create. But this can be a challenge in the beginning. You can get a jumpstart by searching for books or on the internet and then changing the affirmations to fit your specific needs.

When creating or changing your affirmations, remember to keep them positive, in the present tense and personal.

What is important is to create affirmations that speak to you. Affirmations that focus your mind on your goal and motivate you to do the work needed to achieve it.

"In order to earn my black belt, I am going to martial arts class 3 times a week and working out on my own 3 times a week."

2) Say your affirmations out loud every morning.

After you get out of bed, go anywhere where you can walk around, pump your fists into the air and say your affirmation out loud. Do this for 5 to 10 minutes, repeating each affirmation at least three times.

Saying your affirmations out loud while involving your physiology cements your conscious desires into your subconscious mind.

3) Use your affirmations throughout the day

Make time at your breaks, or during lunch to repeat your affirmations. If possible, involve your physiology; if not, at minimum repeat your affirmations out loud.

If you find that what you want is being challenged during the day, use your affirmation to bolster your resolve.

For example, if you have made a commitment to walk a certain amount of steps during the day as part of your "get in shape" goal but a little voice in your head says "It's okay, you can do your steps later" it's time to break out the affirmation. Say your affirmation out loud three times and then get out of your seat and walk!

The key is to use your affirmations throughout your day, making them a part of your conscious and subconscious thinking.

4) Go to sleep thinking about your affirmations.

Say your affirmations softly to yourself or just think about them as you fall to sleep at night. You might even record them to listen to for about fifteen minutes as you are falling asleep. This focuses your mind on your goals as you fall off to dreamland.

Maybe you'll begin dreaming about your goals!

5) Keep track of your behavior.

Keep a notebook or diary and track your thoughts about the behaviors needed to achieve your goal. As you continue to repeat your affirmations, you'll notice that taking action will become easier and easier until one day you will not even think about doing it at all.

Stay with Your Plan

The key is to maintain your focus on your outcome until it becomes a reality. You're making your goal part of your dominant thoughts.

Chapter Eight

The Indomitable Spirit

"Energy and persistence conquer all things."- **Benjamin Franklin**

Bruce Lee was lifting weights early on August 13, 1970. It was a normal part of his morning routine. He hadn't warmed up properly, and before he had finished his first set, he heard a loud popping sound. A tremendous pain in his back accompanied that sound.

For the first few weeks, he tried heat and massage treatments, but his back pain worsened. Finally, he went to seek medical help. After a thorough examination, his doctors told him that his injury was permanent. They told him to rest in bed, and to forget Kung Fu. There was no way he would never kick again.

Bruce had a family that he needed to support, but he could only lay flat on his back. He decided that if he couldn't work out his body, he would work out his mind and for six months he wrote furiously, penning down his own thoughts and methods of the martial arts which he had dedicated his life to.

After six months of rest, he could finally begin exercising again. Six months after that, Bruce was back in shape.

Even though his back hurt for the rest of his life, his indomitable spirit made it possible for him to go to Hong Kong and make his most famous movies.

Never Give Up

"In order to carry a positive action, we must develop here a positive vision." - **Dalai Lama**

In 1989 Ronald Reagan knocked down the Berlin Wall. Although good for world peace (at least at the time) it's falling negatively affected the state of the defense industry in San Diego.

For decades, San Diego had been reliant on the defense industry for its economy. Many of the middle-class families that were part of my martial arts school were also either part of the defense industry or directly affected by it.

The falling of the Berlin Wall caused many of the ones working for the defense department to lose their jobs or move to other parts of the country. In 1992, many local service businesses that had relied on the money from defense contractors, such as restaurants, dry cleaners, and the like, closed down.

The effect on my school's attendance and revenues was devastating. By the early to middle part of 1992, I had lost nearly half of my school's monthly income. At year's end, I was three months behind on my rent.

On December 15th, I received a note from my property owner telling me I had 10 days to pay up or vacate the premises. I had to come up with over $10,000 in 10 days and, for me, that was an enormous pile of money.

For about an hour, that note frightened me out of my wits. I began thinking, "What am I going to do? How am I going to feed my kids? What are my students going to say?"

After that initial hour, I calmed a little and started thinking, "What kind of job can I get?"

I looked at the clock. It was 11:45 AM, time for my favorite class. Noon class was comprised of a group of martial arts fanatics, both men and women, who trained with me every Monday, Wednesday, and Friday. Eight or ten had been training together in this class for years.

When I walked onto the training floor, I looked at their faces. These were people who trusted me, who I had been teaching for years. I didn't know how to tell them that the school was going to close.

I started to open my mouth to speak when the words "Indomitable Spirit" flashed into my consciousness. There was something about those two words that caused me to pause.

The Indomitable Spirit

Possessing an Indomitable Spirit is a tenet or guiding principle of Tang Soo Do and many other martial arts. By definition, a person who possesses an indomitable spirit is "unconquerable and cannot be subdued or overcome." Those who possess this quality will not quit, even when faced with grave danger or even death.

The appearance of those two words in my mind motivated me to keep that news to myself. It was at that moment that I decided to do whatever I needed to do to keep my school open.

I made the decision that I was not going to lie down and quit. I would not let my school close without giving everything inside me to keep it open.

That thought motivated me. The students in that class and all the other classes I taught at my school looked up to me. When they struggled in class or had troubles outside of class, I was the one that would tell them, "Don't give up, you can do it!"

What I thought was what kind of example would I be if I just quit? What would they think, not about me, but about themselves, if I failed?

My fear was they would think, "If he can't succeed, how can I?"

That's why I decided to do everything possible to keep that school open, and I did. I went to work and earned everything I needed, and more, in less than 10 days. That school stayed open for many years after that incident, even after I sold it.

Persistence

"Patience, persistence and perspiration make an unbeatable combination for success." - **Napoleon Hill**

According to the dictionary, persistence is a "firm or obstinate continuance in a course of action despite difficulty or opposition."

One of the most famous stories about persistence, at least in America, was that of Abraham Lincoln. Born in poverty, Abe Lincoln went through several "failures" before becoming one of the best, if not the best, president in all the history of the United States.

Maybe you're not familiar with all the struggles "Honest Abe" went through. The following are most of the major ones.

Very early in his life, a business failure forced Lincoln's family to move from their home in Kentucky to Indiana. A few years later, when he was 9 years old, his mother died. The same year, Lincoln was forced to work to help support his family.

Abe was uneducated, but, through the encouragement of his stepmother, taught himself to read. He eventually read law books. That's how he became a lawyer.

Lincoln joined the army as a captain to fight in the Black Hawk war. He wasn't much of a soldier and left the army.

Lincoln borrowed money from a friend to begin a business. By the end of the year, his business had failed, and he was bankrupt. He spent the next 17 years of his life paying off this debt.

Abe served in the U.S. House of Representatives from 1847 to 1849 but was unpopular with his constituents at home. As a result, he decided not to run for a second term.

Lincoln found the love of his life and became engaged to Anne Rutledge. She died of typhoid fever. After she died, Lincoln became depressed and was bedridden for six months.

He failed to become a speaker of the state legislature. He then tried to get the job of elector and, again, he was shot down.

Abe then sought the job of Illinois land officer, but his party rejected his nomination.

Lincoln ran for U.S. Senator of his state and lost.

Not much later, he sought the Vice-Presidential nomination at his party's national convention. He received less than one hundred votes.

In 1858, Lincoln ran for a seat in the Illinois senate and was part of a series of hotly contested debates with Stephen Douglas. Although Lincoln lost the election, he impressed the Republican Party leaders so much he was able to run for president, which, as you already know, he won.

No matter the rejection and obstacles he faced, Lincoln didn't quit. If he had given up, he would never have won the presidency, and the world would be a much different place today.

Abraham Lincoln possessed the same persistence that Olympic athletes, Navy Seals and Black Belts develop and hone to a razor sharpness. He simply refused to give up, no matter the obstacles he faced.

It's that same indomitable spirit is etched into the consciousness of all successful people. It is a key part of the Black Belt Mindset.

Repetition the Mother of All Habits

If you look at a waterfall, you are watching thousands or even millions of gallons of water streaming over the side of a hill or mountain. A river or stream supplies this fast-flowing avalanche of water.

It's a beautiful sight. All that water coming from who knows where, ending up in a large pond or lake as it spills over the side and to the bottom.

If you were to rewind the hands of time to when that waterfall began, there is a good chance it began as a small trickle. As the rain fell, over time, the water gouged a little path into the earth, giving the water an easier path to follow.

Where the lake or pond is now, there was nothing but flat rock or hard ground. A drop of water would hit the earth below and then another and then another, slowly digging a hole that eventually expanded into the pond or lake that you see at the bottom of the waterfall today.

That river, waterfall and the pond or lake came into being one drop of water at a time.

That's how repetition works.

The behaviors you do today will start to make a path for your brain to follow automatically, pooling into a habit. It's by repeating those behaviors repeatedly that they become your normal behavior.

That's why it is necessary to make your habits out of behaviors that guide you to success. Successful behavior becomes simply what you do.

Why it's Hard to Keep Good Habits

Habits are not always that easy to keep, especially good ones.

For example, when students learn a new form, they'll often "forget" to practice the ones they learned before it. When they take their advancement test, they perform very well on their newest form but poorly on the ones they had learned in the past.

But basics are the building blocks of martial arts. That's why they're called basics. Everything flows from them.

The difference between an average student and one with the Black Belt Mindset is just this. A typical student simply hasn't cultivated a mindset that drives them to persistently practice their basics over and over again.

On the other hand, a black belt is a student who can do their basics well. This is because they consistently practice them repeatedly.

For you to acquire the skills of a black belt, you must practice your basic kicks, your basic punches and blocks, your basic forms over and repeatedly. You need to do this until they become automatic.

Now, while sparring, your techniques seemingly appear out of nowhere, striking like lightning and countering effortlessly. When practicing self-defense, you respond to your attackers' punches or grabs, calmly and flawlessly.

Practicing the basics at whatever you do, whether it's martial arts or project management, over and over again, is what will make you a master.

But the truth is, most people never master anything.

Why?

Because unlike the little stream of water, they have never learned to persist.

Persisting – A History of Success

"Never, never, never give up." - **Winston Churchill**

In Major League Baseball, only three men have hit over 700 homeruns, Barry Bonds, Hank Arron, and Babe Ruth.

While Hank Aaron went on to hit 755 home runs, the second highest homerun record in baseball history, he went 0 for 5 on his first five times at bat with the Milwaukee Braves.

Babe Ruth, of course, was the first player to reach the 700-homerun plateau, hitting 714 homeruns in his career. But

Babe Ruth was also known as a strikeout king. He struck out 1,330 times.

When asked about his propensity for striking out, Babe Ruth said, "Every strike out brings me closer to the next home run."

Nobel Prize winning Albert Einstein didn't speak until he was 4 years old. He didn't read until he was seven. Both his parents and teachers thought him to be slow or sub-normal. In fact, one of his teachers described him as "mentally slow, unsociable, and adrift forever in foolish dreams."

Although initially denied entrance into graduate school, Albert eventually earned his doctoral degree from the Swiss Zurich Polytechnic School, where he came up with the theory of "Relativity" that is still a cornerstone of physics today.

American inventor Thomas Edison accumulated 2,332 worldwide patents and is fifth on the list of total patents in the United States with 1,093. When he was very young, his teachers told him he was "too stupid to learn anything."

Most famous for inventing the light bulb, after having failed to make the light bulb over 1,000 times, a reporter interviewing him asked, "How does it feel to fail 1,000 times?"

Edison reportedly replied, "I haven't failed 1,000 times. I've just found 1,000 ways not to make a light bulb."

Here's the question: why did these people persist while others give up?

I believe it is because they, like everyone else who succeeds, were driven by a compelling vision of their future.

Seeing the Future

"By 1980, I will be the best-known oriental movie star in the United States and will have secured $10 million dollars... And in return, I will give the very best acting I could possibly give every single time I am in front of the camera and I will live in peace and harmony." – **Bruce Lee**

Bruce Lee wrote those words in a letter to himself around 1970. If he would have lived until 1980, I don't have any doubt that he would have easily achieved his goals.

Bruce Lee understood what all successful people understand. How you see your future, what you believe your future can be, is what you will become.

If You Wish Upon a Star

"All our dreams can come true, if we have the courage to pursue them." - **Walt Disney**

Walt Disney could have been a monumental failure. In fact, early in his adult life, Walt Disney was fired by a newspaper editor because "he lacked imagination and had no good ideas."

After creating Mickey Mouse, he was told that the idea of a cartoon about a mouse was "one of the dumbest things anybody had ever heard of".

When Walt Disney visited the World's Fair, he thought how sad it was that it would soon close, and nobody would be able to visit it anymore. That's when he came up with the idea of having a year-round theme park.

Before he built Disneyland, Walt had started several businesses that failed and ended in bankruptcy. 302 bankers and the city of Anaheim rejected his proposal for Disneyland initially, saying that it would only attract riffraff.

Of course, on July 17, 1955, Disneyland was open to the public and Mickey Mouse has become one of the most recognized figures in the world.

What you might not know is that in 1963, Walt Disney started buying up land in the Orlando Florida area to build Disney World.

It was to be the ideal place for his new dream of a larger version of Disneyland that he named Disney World. He wanted to avoid the land speculation and the skyrocketing prices that would follow if anyone found out about his dream.

By 1966, he had successfully acquired the land he wanted for his new project. That same year, after years of chain smoking, doctors diagnosed Walt with lung cancer.

His prognosis was grim. He knew he was going to die.

Shortly before his death, he invited a reporter to see him. During the interview, the reporter asked, "Mr. Disney, how does it feel to never be able to see Disney World completed?"

With a smile, Walt looked at the reporter and replied, "I do know what it will look like. Disney World was completed in my mind long before we ever started to build it."

A Star Is Born

Born in Berlin, Germany in 1970, both of Audra McDonald's parents worked in education. Her mother as an administrator of a university, her father as a principle at a high school for the U.S. Army.

After their tour in Germany, they moved to Fresno, California.

As a young girl in Fresno, she would practice saying her Tony Award acceptance speech into her hairbrush. She would go into her closet and walk out to the applause of her audience of teddy bears and dolls.

Her dream was to become a famous entertainer on Broadway but, after high school, she instead attended the prestigious Juilliard School of Arts, learning classical music.

While at Julliard she became homesick and depressed, and she attempted suicide. She spent the next month in a mental health facility. During that time, she reconnected with her dream and, in her words, "got better".

After returning to Julliard, she graduated in 1993. Using what she had learned there, she worked diligently to find a job that would fulfil her dream on Broadway.

A year later, she won her first Tony Award for her role in Carousel.

Since then, she's had several TV and movie appearances as well. Most recently Disney's 2017 remake of Beauty and the Beast.

A Stroke of Luck?

As of 2014, Phil Mickelson is one of only 15 golfers to win at least three of the four professional majors. He has also won the Masters three times.

Born in 1970 and almost before he could walk, Phil started practicing hitting the ball with his dad. After watching Gary Player win the Masters in 1974, he became a golf fanatic, telling his parents that would be him winning the Masters someday.

After graduating high school, Phil went on to Arizona State University where he started to turn his dream into a reality. There he won three NCAA individual championships and three Haskins Awards.

After becoming a pro, Phil won the Master's in 2004 and 2006. While preparing to compete in the 2010 U.S. Open at Pebble Beach, he started feeling aches in his joints. Finally, when he almost couldn't get out of bed, he went to the doctor and was diagnosed with psoriatic arthritis.

Phil decided he would not let this, or anything else, stop him from playing the game he loved. That year he went on to win at the 'Shell Houston Open,' placing him at the number three spot on the world ranking list.

Later that year, he won his third Master's, despite his illness. As of the writing of this book, Phil is still playing the game he loves.

The Indomitable Spirit

Bruce Lee, Walt Disney, Audra McDonald, and Phil Mickelson all possessed an indomitable spirit. Their spirit was fortified by their vision of what their life would be like.

Because they already "knew" what life had in store for them, they could persevere even under the toughest circumstances.

So can you.

Developing a Positive Vision

"In order to carry a positive action, we must develop here a positive vision." - **Dalai Lama**

The movie "Rush" is about two 1976 Formula 1 racecar drivers, James Hunt and Niki Lauda. These two developed a fascinating rivalry that was played out in the media around the world.

In one scene, the character James Hunt (played by Chris Hemsworth) is laying on his back with a steering wheel imagining going through the racecourse in his mind. After being questioned by his companions about what he's doing, he responds that it's a "new idea" the crew thought could use to help him win.

What James Hunt was using is known as creative visualization.

Creative Visualization is simply using your imagination to create your perfect future outcome.

The Origins of Creative Visualization

While it might have been a new idea to James Hunt, creative visualization, as we know it today, has been around since the mid-1800s. American author Wallace Wattles writes about it in his book "The Science of Getting Rich." In this book, he tells his readers that it is "one of the best ways to reach your goals".

But this wasn't a new idea even then. Wallace Wattles was part of the "New Thought movement." They took the idea of creative visualization from the ancient Hindu Monistic theory of the Universe.

Since then, creative visualization has been talked about and adapted by people from every walk of life. In fact, many celebrities, athletes, entrepreneurs have used creative visualization successfully to pursue and achieve their goals and dreams.

For example, Arnold Schwarzenegger talks about how he used creative visualization to first win the Mr. Universe competition, then become a famous movie actor and ultimately become the Governor of California.

Will Smith has talked about his use of creative visualization in developing his career as has the world's richest woman, Oprah Winfrey, the former CEO of Apple Computers Steve Jobs, and the founder of Microsoft and one of the world's richest men Bill Gates.

As you can see, no one just falls into success. It takes a compelling vision and hard work.

Lots of hard work.

Like Walt Disney, Audra McDonald and Phil Mickelson and any successful person, it's this compelling vision that will drive you to the future of your dreams.

Like a magnet, creative visualization will pull you to where you want to go.

How Does Creative Visualization Work?

Psychologists divide your brain into two sections, known as the right and the left hemisphere. This theory is based on the work of Nobel Prize winning neuropsychologist Roger W. Sperry and is best known as the theory of the lateralization of brain function.

According to this theory, each side of your brain controls two distinctly different thinking.

Your left brain is your logical brain. It is incredibly detailed oriented. It uses words and language and can comprehend complex subjects like math and science.

Your left brain is reality based. It uses its amazing powers to form strategies to keep you safe.

While you use both sides of your brain simultaneously, according to this theory, your creative imagination is in your right brain.

Using your right brain, you can create images of your desired outcome. These images link your two hemispheres together, allowing you to use all the amazing tools available to you.

Creative Visualization at Work

There have been scientific studies that involve creative visualization. The most famous is the by L. V. Clark who was a psychology professor at Wayne State University. His goal was to understand the power of the imagination, so he designed and conducted a two-week study of high school basketball players[10].

In the experiment, he divided the athletes into three groups. To measure the effectiveness of the process in each group, at the beginning of the experiment, he recorded how many times each player could make free throws.

He set up his experiment like this:

The first group (the control group) only followed their usual routine. They did nothing extra to improve their free throw skills.

The second group put in an hour a day of extra practice time shooting free-throws.

The third group also put in extra practice time. The difference was they used their time imaging or visualizing making perfect free-throw shots. They did no "extra, real" physical practice.

The first group (the "do-nothings") performed as expected. Their percentage of shooting free throws didn't change or improve. They made the same average number of free throws as they did at the start of the experiment.

The second group who practiced making the free throws improved their free-throw percentages by an average of a full 24%. All that practice made an enormous difference!

The third group who only imagined making perfect free-throw shots improved their free-throw skills by a whopping 23%! Even though they did no "extra, real" physical practice, their free throw effectiveness improved nearly as much as the group who spent all their time "actually practicing".

Since then, Clark's original experiment has been duplicated many times by other researchers, with very similar results. These scientific studies are clear demonstrations of the amazing power of creative visualization.

Back to Your Burning Desire

Before going on to Black Belt Mind Secret # 9, review the desire declaration you created.

As you review it, ask yourself, "What is it what I really want to accomplish? "

Make sure you have a clear idea of what you want before going on to Black Belt Mind Secret # 9.

Black Belt Mind Secret # 9 – Creating Your Compelling Future

Now that you know your burning desire, you're going to use creative visualization to turn your desire declaration into your compelling future.

You're going to use the amazing power of creative visualization to create your compelling future. The following model is a visualization process you can start with.

While this process is great in the beginning, in order for this to work for you, it needs to be tailored to your specific outcome. This means that as you become more comfortable with this process, you need to adapt it to your personality. The more personal you make it, the more effective it will be.

The Visualization Process

Find a comfortable place where you can sit and relax undisturbed. Make sure you turn off all of your electronic leashes and let the people in your life know that you need at least 30 undisturbed minutes.

Once you are in your place, sit down and close your eyes. Using Black Belt Mind Secret # 4, belly breathing, take a deep breath in through your nose. As you let it out slowly, just allow your mind and body to relax as you just allow all the cares and worries of the day to slip away.

Continue to take in breaths for a few minutes, bringing in calm and relaxation with every breath in, and letting out all your cares and worries with every breath out.

Now that you are relaxed, imagine yourself in the future. As you imagine yourself in the future, also imagine that you have accomplished the goal you have been working on for so long.

In your mind, describe what it is you have accomplished in vivid detail.

If it is a financial goal, imagine the amount of money.

If it is a physical goal, imagine what you are able to accomplish with your body, what your body looks like.

If it's a professional goal, imagine the new position you are in or what your business is now accomplishing.

If it's a spiritual goal, imagine how you feel now that you have climbed up to this new plane.

Whatever your goal, allow this image of you achieving your goal to grow larger in your mind. Imagine yourself as already having accomplished it. As you do this, let this image begin to take over your consciousness. Allow it to become your reality.

Now, as this image takes over your consciousness, begin to involve your representational systems and your sub modalities.

Starting with your visual representational system, zoom in and notice, really notice, your expression, how do you appear?

Are you grinning from ear to ear?

Do you have a quiet look of contentment?

Is there a certain gleam in your eyes?

Are people reacting to you differently? How are they reacting to you?

Deeply examine how you look, what you are wearing, the people who are around you and allow this image to grow in your mind.

Now, using your kinesthetic representational system, notice your posture, how you are sitting or standing. Notice how you feel now that you've accomplished your goal.

Do you have a feeling of confidence surrounding you?

If you are standing, is your head held high and your back straight?

Is your breathing slow and rhythmic?

Are you jumping up and down with joy?

Using your auditory representational system, what sounds are going through your mind now that your dream has become a reality?

Is there a voice telling you something, congratulating you on a job well done?

What are the people around you telling you? Are they encouraging you, congratulating you?

As you experience their reactions, notice the state that you're in. How does that make you feel?

As you enjoy this state in this wonderful future of yours, ask yourself, "Was all the sacrifice and commitment and dedication that it took to get here worth it?"

Listen as a voice shouts, "Of course it was worth it!"

As that voice echoes in your mind, see yourself overcoming the obstacles that are in your way. Hear yourself as you say your affirmations over and over again, chipping away at those barriers that used to hold you back.

Watch as you go through the processes you've learned in this book cause those obstacles to crumble and fade."

Also, notice all the naysayers, the negative people who told you that you weren't good enough, that you could never stick to it, and that you couldn't do it. Notice how all those negative people just disappear, fade away.

Notice how your beliefs have shifted. You now have a new set of beliefs to build upon. Beliefs that empower you, that bring out the very best in you.

Go back to when you first started your quest, where you were weeks, months, even years before. Notice how far you've come along your path to success, how you homed in like a laser to accomplish your goal.

Nothing could stand in your way! You made no excuses. You just did the work you needed to do to accomplish your goal.

This allowed you to overcome any and all barriers that popped up along the way.

Take a deep breath and allow yourself to feel this sense of pride in your accomplishments. Allow your entire being to feel good about yourself and what you've done.

Let your emotions soar! Let your mind and body rejoice!

Now open your eyes and bask in the feelings all around you.

Allow yourself to enjoy your compelling future NOW!

Note: If you'd like, you can read your script into a recording device and play it back as you go through this exercise. This can help you with the process, especially in the beginning.

From Burning Desire to Compelling Future

You have just turned your burning desire into a compelling future using the amazing power of creative visualization. This image of your compelling future will give you the inspiration you need to get up off the couch and do whatever it takes to achieve your goals.

Now, let's see how Black Belts turn this compelling vision into the Black Belt Mindset so you can become truly unstoppable.

Chapter Nine

Transformation

"If you wish to control others, you must first control yourself." - **Miyamoto Musashi, The Book of the Five Rings**

Choi Young-Eui was born in Japanese occupied Korea on July 27, 1923. When he was 9 years old, his parents sent him to live in to live with his sister in Manchuria. There he had his first taste of the martial arts, learning Kempo from one of his sister's farm hands.

The Japanese occupation of Korea had begun in 1910 and would continue until the end of World War II. As the war in the Pacific heated up, the Japanese began conscripting young men from its many occupied countries, including Korea. Choi Young-Eui was one of those conscripts.

He moved to Japan in 1938. The Japanese war machine soon selected him for aviation school.

Being young, he felt pride in being chosen for such an honor and changed his name to Masutatsu Oyama, better known in his later years as Mas.

But there was a problem. They quickly discovered that Mas wasn't a gifted pilot and the Japanese air school let him go. Still wanting to serve his newly adopted country, he enlisted in the Imperial Army and was sent to the Butokukai, a Japanese Military academy.

The Butokukai had one of Japan's best unarmed combat schools. This allowed Mas to continue his martial arts training. Here he practiced boxing and judo.

In town, he started training at the school of the Okinawan Karate Master, Gichin Funakoshi[11]. He was a talented student and by the time he was 21, he had earned his fourth-degree black belt.

In the war, he never left for combat. At the war's end, he was, like every other conscript, let go from the imperial army. He also discovered that because of his Korean heritage, the very ethnocentric Japanese no longer welcomed him. This made it nearly impossible for him to find work.

Bitter from the loss of many of his friends and comrades, he began randomly attacking U.S. servicemen attached to the military occupation forces in Japan. While he later confessed that this type of cheap revenge, hitting these servicemen when they weren't expecting it made him feel better about the death of his companions, it did nothing to improve his martial arts skills. In fact, the only thing it resulted in was him spending time in jail.

About this time, Mas had also begun practicing Goju Ry, training under So Nei Chu, who was a fellow Korean master. He was known for both his physical and spiritual strength and was one of the most knowledgeable Masters of Goju Ryu in Japan. He was a living model of what Mas thought a martial artist should be like.

Simultaneously, he met Eiji Yoshikawa, the author of the novel Musashi, a book loosely based on the life and exploits of Japan's most famous Samurai warrior, Miyamoto Musashi. In this book, Mas learned about the Samurai Bushido code. After reading the book, Mas decided he would dedicate his life to living in line with this code.

Mas Oyama knew he wanted to become like Miyamoto Musashi, the perfect Samurai Warrior. Master So supported his idea and urged him to take the action needed to make his goal a reality, so he did.

The action he took was to climb Mt. Minobu, the same mountain where his idol Musashi had originally compiled "The Book of Five Rings" and train in the wilderness. He felt that through rigorous training of mind, body and spirit, he could transform himself into the same type of person as his idol Musashi, an unstoppable Samurai Warrior.

By anyone's estimate, his training was almost superhuman. Mas would begin training at five in the morning, running up the steep mountain slopes. He would lift large rocks hundreds of times. He performed his kata (Karate forms) at least a hundred times each day and would practice his basic techniques, kicking, punching and blocking hundreds, if not thousands, of times.

He wanted to spend three years in the wilderness, but unfortunately his sponsor stopped supporting him after 14 months and Mas returned to civilization.

After returning, Mas Oyama was the first martial artist to win the open Championship in the Japanese National Martial Arts Championships since the end of War II. His training had made him into such an exceptional physical specimen that no one could even come close to beating him.

But he was still dissatisfied and unhappy. He greatly improved his physical skills, but he did not believe he was of the same mold as his idol, Musashi. To him, the only way to reach this level was to spend another eighteen months in the wilderness. So, with new sponsorship brought on by his new found fame, he climbed Mt. Kiyozum to finish his training.

This time, he began training twelve hours a day. His physical training was even more fanatical. He would stand in a nearly freezing waterfall while finding and breaking stones with his bare hands. Over and over, he would kick and punch trees with his feet and hands. He would also jump over rapidly growing flax plants hundreds of times each day.

To develop his mind and spirit, Mas would sit under an ice-cold waterfall while meditating on Zen koans[12]. In the evening, he would read various Buddhist writings and sit in the lotus or Zazen position and meditate, searching for enlightenment.

As you might imagine, this time when he returned, Mas was a changed man. He was so physically powerful that he could drive his hand through a dozen roofing tiles as easily as an outdoorsman could split firewood with a new, sharpened ax. After wrestling a bull to the ground, he used his hand to chop one of its horns in half and then killed it with a single blow to the head.

He became the founder of the Japanese Kyokushin Karate[13] system, which is known for its full contact fighting. This system has developed some of the best full contact Karateka in the world. Mas led his students by example. He was the toughest of the tough, the epitome of a full contact fighter. He took on all challengers, knocking out many of them with a single blow5.

But the genuine change came in his demeanor. No longer was he compelled to randomly attack U.S. servicemen. Instead, he was calm, tranquil, and extremely focused. People who encountered him said his mere presence could calm all who came near him.

One time, when questioned about maintaining his tranquility while involved in such a violent activity, Mas responded, "Karate is not a game. It is not a sport. It is not even a system of self-defense. Karate is half physical exercise and half spiritual. The karateka who has given the necessary years of exercise and meditation is a tranquil person. He is unafraid. He can be calm in a burning building."

Through his sojourn in the wilderness, Mas Oyama transformed himself into a perfect image of the type of Samurai Warrior depicted in Eiji Yoshikawa's novel. One whose mind is his ultimate weapon.

Through this transformational process, he developed the mindset that all martial artists aspire to gain, but very few achieve, the Black Belt Mindset. With this mindset Mas Oyama's mind became completely calm and focused and, as a result, he was totally unstoppable.

You're probably saying, "Even if I had the inclination to follow in Mas Oyama's footsteps (which I don't), I don't have three years to spend in the wilderness." The good news is you don't need to. You can cultivate a similar mindset by utilizing the methods you've discovered in this book right in the convenience of your own home, a mindset that can take you from where you are to where you want to be.

The Path to Transformation

"There is nothing outside of yourself that can ever enable you to get better, stronger, richer, quicker, or smarter. Everything is within. Everything exists. Seek nothing outside of yourself." - **Miyamoto Musashi, The Book of Five Rings**

Steps to Transformation

It's important to note that the path that Mas Oyama took to transform himself into the ultimate Samurai Warrior didn't just appear overnight out of nowhere. It took him years of training until he got lucky and had the simultaneous influence of So Nei Chu and Eiji Yoshikawa.

Now, before I go on, I must give you the best definition of luck I've ever heard. "Luck is when opportunity meets preparedness."

Mas had spent years preparing himself for this opportunity and when it came up, he was ready to take advantage of it.

That's the importance of doing the exercises in this book. They will get you ready for your "lucky" break. Once you have prepared yourself, you can use the process in this chapter to move you from where you are now to where you want to be. You too, can become unstoppable.

The Transformation Process

By going through the exercises in this book, you have already prepared yourself for the transformational process. The following five steps will make this process easier and, even more important, repeatable.

1. What Do You Want to Change?

"For the past 33 years, I have looked in the mirror every morning and asked myself: 'If today were the last day of my life, would I want to do what I am about to do today?' And whenever the answer has been 'No' for too many days in a row, I know I need to change something." - **Steve Jobs**

Why did Mas Oyama decide to go into the wilderness? I believe he went because, after looking at what he wanted for his life, he came to understand that if he kept going in the direction he was headed, he would never become the kind of martial artist he sincerely wanted to be.

It was the difference between his values and who he was that disturbed him. This inner disturbance made him want to change.

What is it that disturbs you about where you are in life right now? Is it your physical health, your finances, what you do for a living, your relationship?

If you're not sure, go back to Black Belt Mind Secret #1 to get a better grasp of your values. What are you falling short of? What is making you feel extremely uncomfortable?

Only by understanding what disturbs you at a deep level will you ever be able to inspire yourself to take the next step, which is…

2. Decide What You Do Want.

"It is in your moments of decision that your destiny is shaped."
- **Tony Robbins**

While being dissatisfied is a good starting point, dissatisfaction doesn't provide you with any direction. Anyone can be unhappy with where they are presently. In fact, this is the default mode of most people and if you ask them, they will gladly tell you how unhappy they are.

When you talk with these people, you'll find that they have an external locus of control. They believe that they are controlled by forces beyond their control. They tell you that the government, the economy or some conspiracy is what is keeping them from getting what they want.

Achievers not only know what they don't want, they also know what they do want. Mas Oyama knew he wanted to become a martial arts master like his idol, Miyamoto Musashi. The reason he wanted to become like Musashi was because, at least to him, Musashi was the perfect Samurai Warrior, the model of martial arts perfection.

So, the question is, what is it you want?

Do you want to become a black belt, a master, a successful businessperson, a millionaire, a teacher?

If you're struggling with this, use Black Belt Mind Secret #7 to help you home in on what you want.

Once you have decided what you want, you need to take the next step…

3. Create a Plan

"First comes thought; then organization of that thought, into ideas and plans; then transformation of those plans into reality."

- Napoleon Hill

Now that you have figured out what you don't want and what you do want, what do you need to get there? What tools will you use, what people will you consult, what path will you take?

It's not enough to want something; you need a plan to get it. Now that you know where you want to go, you need to create a map that will take you there or at least get you started in the right direction.

That's why Mas Oyama brought the Book of the 5 Rings into the wilderness with him. It was to be his step-by-step map of how to become the ultimate Samurai Warrior.

The best way to create your map of how to get to where you want to go is to, as Stephen Covey pointed out in his book "The 7 Habits of Highly Effective People", "Begin with the End in Mind". Once you've figured out what it is you want (step 2) you work backwards until you have a step-by-step map of how to get there.

For example, if you want to become a black belt, you need to decide what style you want to learn. Then you need to decide how much time and effort you're committed to putting into this goal and who you want to train with

If you want a certain level of income, you decide on that level of income and then figure out how you can develop that level of income. What are you going to do to achieve that level of income? How long is it going to take you? Who else has achieved this level of income? How did they go about it?

If you want to be at a certain fitness level, what does that appear like to you? Is it a certain weight, a certain pant or dress size? Is it the ability to do a certain type of exercise or run a certain distance? Who can you use as a role model?

Now write out a step-by-step plan of how you are going to achieve your goal. Just like Mas Oyama, having your plan on paper will make your goal real to you. It also gives you a structure to return to when you need guidance or motivation.

It doesn't matter what it is you want to achieve, what matters is that you know what it is and have a plan to achieve it. Once you have your plan, you need to write it down.

Now you can move to the next step...

4. Take Action

For of all sad words of tongue or pen, the saddest are these: "It might have been!" - **Maud Muller**

I've talked to many people who are going to take martial arts, create an app, run a marathon, start a business, get into shape, write a book, or a myriad of other admirable things. These people have great ideas. Many of these people have even created a plan that will help them make their dream a reality, but most people never even come close to achieving what they set out to do.

So why is it that so few people's plans ever come to fruition?

The real problem with most people is they fail to take action.

Mas Oyama decided he wanted to be a Samurai Warrior fashioned in the same mold as Miyamoto Musashi. He also decided that the only way he could become like his idol would be to "walk a mile in his shoes".

That's why Mas climbed Mt. Minobu and trained like a fanatic. He knew he could read about Musashi's exploits 24 hours a day, 7 days a week, and become nothing close to his ideal of a Samurai Warrior. While reading might change the way he felt, it would never change who he was. It would take action to transform his mind and body, making him a calm yet deadly warrior.

In his mind, he could only do this by climbing the mountain and training alone in an extreme fashion. He believed that step by step, he could become the person he wanted to become.

His first steps reinforced his belief that what he wanted to do was possible. Then, inch by inch, it became more and more possible until, when he finally came back from his first wilderness experience, he had transformed his body into an undefeatable fighting machine.

That's why it's so important to take the first step on whatever plans you've made and then repeat taking the action steps daily that you've set for yourself. Because you can only become what you are committed to taking action to become. Your first action steps will then begin to build the belief you need to continue on the path you have chosen.

If you are having trouble with your belief, you can use Black Belt Mind Secrets #2 and 3.

So, what action do you need to take? What one step will move you toward your goal today? Once you've taken action, you can move to the next step...

5. Review Your Progress

The odds of your plan taking you straight down the path to your goal are slim to none. No matter how good your plan is, you are going to run into roadblocks and detours along the way.

When Mas first started out on his quest, his goal was to train in the wilderness for three years. At first, a fellow student named Yashiro accompanied him. For whatever reason, Yashiro wasn't as dedicated to the quest as Mas. After six months decided that this wasn't for him and he took off in the middle of the night, never to return.

This left Mas completely isolated. He confessed to his mentor, Master So, that he wanted badly to return at times, just to have a conversation.

After only fourteen months, his benefactor couldn't afford to sponsor him anymore. This forced Mas to return to civilization. His plan had officially been foiled.

Even though he had reached a level of physical competence that allowed him to win the Karate Championship, he felt he still hadn't reached the level of mental and spiritual competence he had set out to find.

The same goes for you. Sometimes things just will not work out the way you wanted. You'll find as you review your progress you may be happy with some things you've accomplished but, like Mas, you might still find you are lacking in other areas. That's the purpose of the review; to help you understand what still needs to be done and to adjust your actions so you can achieve it.

Mas understood this and I believe this fueled him to enter and win the Karate Championship. He understood it would provide him with enough notoriety to attract another sponsor, and it did. As a result, Mas Oyama climbed Mt. Kiyozum and finished his quest.

Elizabeth Kubler Ross once said, "People are like stained glass windows. They sparkle and shine when the sun is out, but when the darkness sets in, their true beauty is revealed only if there is a light from within."

This is what happened with Mas and is what can happen to you when you follow this process. It can help you find the light you need to guide you along your path, no matter how dark the journey becomes.

Using this process and the Black Belt Mind Secrets you've learned in this book; you can move from where you are now to where you want to be. All it takes is a little time, determination, and practice.

Chapter Ten

The Real Secret

"If you spend too much time thinking about a thing, you'll never get it done." - **Bruce Lee**

Over the years, people have continued to ask me, "What is the best martial arts system to practice?"

I used to reply by asking, well what do you want to use it for, self-defense, fitness? Do you want to learn how to kick and punch or to grapple?

Then I'd listen to their answers.

After all these years, I don't go through this drill anymore, instead I tell them it's the one that you practice.

As Bruce Lee said, *"I fear not the man who has practiced 10,000 kicks once, but I fear the man who has practiced one kick 10,000 times."*

Nothing could be truer.

Someone who has practiced one kick 10,000 times is going to be awfully good at it.

When it comes to martial arts, or anyone else, skills will only become proficient with practice.

Mastery of anything is about practice.

This all starts in your mind. What you keep in your mind becomes a reality.

As Earl Nightingale once said, *"All you have to do is know where you're going. The answers will come to you of their own accord."*

In this book, I exposed you to Nine Black Belt Mind Secrets.

I also gave you a 5-step process to use, to take you in the direction of your goals and dreams.

But, like the practice of martial arts, this isn't a onetime scenario where you perform a technique once and it's available anytime you need it.

You will need to practice the secrets you've learned repeatedly until they become second nature.

Only then will you have mastered the Black Belt Mindset.

Let me end with this...

I hope this book has been both interesting and helpful and I wish you only success, now and for the rest of your life.

Wil Dieck
September 29, 2014

About the Author

Are you feeling a little lost and unsure of your path in life?

We've got just the solution for you!

Meet Wil Dieck, the mastermind behind Mindful Mind Hacking.

With his extensive background in hypnotherapy, NLP, martial arts, and mindfulness, he's got the tools you need to unlock your true potential and create the life you've always dreamed of.

And who doesn't want that?

Wil's forty years of experience have helped countless clients and students achieve their goals and break free from any barriers holding them back.

So, whether you're looking for online courses, books, one-on-one coaching, or group presentations, Wil's got you covered.

Don't wait any longer - visit the Contact page on Mindful MindHacking.comand start hacking into your success today!

Other Books by Wil Dieck

Mastering the Mind, Body and Spirit: Secrets of Black Belt Peak Performance

Modern Mindfulness: A Beginners Guide on How to Find Peace and Happiness in a Busy World

Subliminal Success: How to Harness the Power of Your Subconscious Mind

Mindful Mastery: Find Focus, Get Unstuck, and Drop Into the Peak Performance Zone

NLP - UNLOCK YOUR DREAMS: A Beginners Guide to Neuro Linguistic Programming

1. Wilhelm Maximilian Wundt (16 August 1832 – 31 August 1920) was a German physician, physiologist, philosopher, and professor. He is recognized as one of the founding figures of modern psychology. You can learn more about him at http://www.wilhelmwundt.com/

2. The K'ihap (Korean) or Kaai (Japanese) is a short yell made before, during, or after a technique.

3. Jae C. Shin was later sponsored by Chuck to come to the U.S. He went on to establish the U.S. Tang Soo Do Federation.

4. You can read more about this effect on page 40 in the book "On Combat: The Psychology and Physiology of Deadly Conflict in War and in Peace" by Dave Grossman, Loren W. Christensen.

5. You can read more about the evolutionary effect of fear on page 63 in the book, "Phobias: Fighting the Fear" by Helen Sau.

6. You can read more about Atkinson's experiments in the 1969 book "Fear of failure" by Robert Charles Birney, Harvey Burdick and Richard Collier Teevan

7. For more information about the fear of success, read "Overcoming the Fear of Success" by Martha Friedman.

8. Napoleon Hill is considered one of the greatest self-help authors of all time. If you haven't read his book "Think and Grow Rich" I would highly recommend it.

9. You can learn more about Tony Robbins and his philosophy in his book "Awaken the Giant Within" as well as his many other books and audio programs.

10. Clark LV. "Effect of mental practice on the development of a certain motor skill." Research Quarterly, v31 n4 (Dec 1960):560-569]

11. Gichin Funakoshi is the founder of Shotokan Karate-Do, which is perhaps the most widely known style of karate in the world today. Born in Okinawa, he moved to Japan in 1922 and is widely recognized as the "father of modern karate".

12. A Zen koan is used in Zen Buddhism to help beginners meditate. Its purpose is to be thought about long enough to exhaust the conscious, analytic mind so the unconscious mind can develop an appropriate, intuitive response.

13. You can find more information about Mas Oyama and Kyokushin Karate at http://www.masutatsuoyama.com/

Made in the USA
Columbia, SC
14 July 2024

e53e78da-9188-4826-8066-4aa83c0036fbR01